WITHDRAWN

MRS BEETON'S
Game
COOKERY

MRS BEETON'S
Game
COOKERY

WARD LOCK

Designed by Ann Thompson
Consultant Editor Bridget Jones

Photography by Jhon K████
Home economist Stella Joyce
Stylist Valerie Key████

Illustrations: pages
18–19 Owain Bell
22–38 John Wood████
all other illustrations
by David Hopki████
Hand lettering on ja████
by Tony Spaul.

Text filmset in 13/14pt Bembo by Columns of Reading
Printed and bound in Spain by Cayfosa

Beeton, Mrs, 1836–1865
Mrs Beeton's game cookery.
1. Food: Game dishes, — Recipes
I. Title
641.6'91

ISBN 0-7063-6805-3

Contents

'fit for beings better than men'

Introduction

by Michael Barry

This book is long overdue! It is clear and practical and it doesn't take us and our knowledge (or lack of it) for granted. The introduction to 'Salmis of Pheasant' is an excellent example: "Salmis is the term used for a dish which has two cooking methods; the first is roasting, the second braising or stewing in a rich brown sauce, usually with the addition of wine". There, in a couple of lines, is all you need to know, not only to help do the job, but to impress your friends with your culinary knowledge. This is such a welcome change from the usual run of the game cookery books, many of which seem to start from the premise that everyone has hot and cold running gamekeepers.

I suppose this approach is commonly adopted because we British have a long and romantic relationship with game, its catching and its cooking. For example, one of the most enduring of our legends is that of Robin Hood and his merry men, roasting the King's venison around an open fire in Sherwood. Popular traditional songs, like the Lincolnshire Poacher with his 'delight on a shiny night in the season of the year', celebrate in another way the acquisition of game in less than legal style. We even talk of 'a hunters moon' when that satellite fills the autumn sky with radiance enough to see our way across the game coverts and fields in the concealing dark. In addition to these romantic traditions, what used to be thought the best cookery joke is about game . . . first catch your hare! Not quite as self evident as it seems, 'catching' a hare is the term used for removing the iridescent membrane under the skin before cutting it up. This is a refinement usually attributed to Mrs Beeton although I can find no trace of it in her original book.

However, Mrs Beeton was a real game enthusiast. In the first edition of her *Book of Household Management*, Mrs Beeton quoted the famous French chef Brillat Savarin on the subject of game; to be precise, on the matter of roast pheasant. The master, she noted with approval, believed a properly roast pheasant "is fit for beings better than men". Not a modest statement, but one that reflected the enormous traditional enthusiasm for game, furred or feathered. This book brings that enthusiasm right up to date – there is a recipe for a barbecue of rabbit alongside the instructions for roasting a haunch of venison should the outlaw spirit take you. Here you will find traditional raised game pie and potted meat as well as exotic recipes for Spanish braised partridge, the Polish national dish, Bigos (game with sauerkraut), or hare marinated in the style of a famous Finnish Marshal.

Another reason to recommend this modern guide to game, is our unfamiliarity and nervousness with the subject. While our cooking traditions for game go back countless centuries, so too does a certain fear of game, or at least of its acquisition and preparation. In mediaeval times, whole tracts of land were set aside for royal or noble hunting forests, that is, for hunting game and penalty for a commoner infringing this privileged hunting ground was death. The New Forest was created by the newly arrived Norman Kings for just this purpose of the chase. I like to believe (and the evidence from royal menus bears this out) that the appeal was not only the excitement of the hunt but the pleasure of the palate.

Perhaps the best reason to welcome this cookbook is the most obvious one – game tastes good! It has succulence, intense flavour and a depth of richness that no other food manages . . . worth having a forest aside set for its benefit. Game offers a range of flavours and textures far wider than domestic meats. We live on three kinds of meat and, except for Christmas, one kind of poultry – not a wide choice looked at in this way, is it? In this guide to game cooking you will find recipes and detailed preparation instructions for no less than nine different kinds of game birds and three types of meat. Some are more easy to find than others and, I have to confess, some more easy to love, but for variety, flavour and good eating the book abounds with ideas.

Now that some game (venison in particular) is farmed it is much cheaper as well as far more readily available. Some of the multiple supermarkets stock a range of game birds and many game dealers are starting to provide for this new demand. The really good news is that, whether farmed or wild, all game is a particularly healthly food. It is low in fat (beware of putting too much back on with larding and barding) and quite free of all the hormone additives, growth promoters and everyday threats of grim infections that result from intensive rearing. So . . . a healthy, easy and delicious range of foods is just waiting to be cooked and savoured with the help of this new book on an old topic.

Move over Robin, I fancy a little of that venison.

Wines for Game

by Robin Young

Historical tradition dictates an almost monogamous marriage between game and red Burgundy. Game eaters drink red Burgundy. Red Burgundy drinkers eat game. It has been as simple as that. This orthodoxy derives, though, from a time when the choice of wines available was only a fraction of that which is offered now – and from an era when wine nomenclature was by no means as strict or exact as the disciplined regime that now applies. The red Burgundies which Mrs Beeton would have considered suitable accompaniment to game dishes were, in fact, almost invariably 'improved' with liberal doses of heavy, anonymous wines brought up covertly from the Rhône. In poor vintages, of which red Burgundy still has approximately two in every three years, this helped Burgundy producers imitate the style and weight which their unaided efforts could achieve in only the most favourable circumstances. Both wine making and game cookery have continued to evolve since Mrs Beeton's day, so that now the rules of matching game and wine have to be revised and liberalized.

It is a sensible guideline whenever choosing wine, to relate the price of the bottle to the cost of the food on the plate. By and large, though some wines are better bargains than others, you get what you pay for. The higher quality and more expensive the meat, the finer the wine that should accompany it, so that roasting birds qualify for top quality and stews or casseroles are sufficiently served with basic, good-quality wines.

Rabbit, though never to be despised, ranks low in the league of game, by price and excellence. The simple flavour and satisfying succulence of rabbit is best suited by the direct flavours of relatively simple wine rather than by the complexity of fine wine. The lighter the dish, the lighter the wine; with a barbecue of rabbit, for example, a good red French *vin de pays*, drunk young and, if preferred, even chilled will be completely adequate.

For more elaborate roasts something slightly more substantial would be more appropriate: young Rioja; a lively, bumptious Beaujolais; juicy Cabernet Franc from the Loire; or a zesty, bright Chianti. For stews move up to peppery Côtes-du-Rhone, the younger Portuguese red wines, and inexpensive varietal red wines – Cabernet Sauvignon especially – from Bulgaria, New Zealand or Australia.

Wild pigeon takes relatively modest wines as well, but because its flavour is stronger it should be treated to an extra degree of vinous strength and intensity. It would be an exceptional *vin de pays* that would work well at all; the Loire red should be Chinon or Bourgeuil rather than lighter, racier Saumur Champigny; take Beaujolais-Villages and Côtes-du-Rhône Villages in preference to the simple appellation wines; or try some of the richly fruity and vigorous Italian wines such as Dolcetto, Montepulciano d'Abruzzo or Rubesco Torgiano.

Quail

The quail we eat today are farmed, and especially good with these delicate little birds are the light, febrile and nervy Pinot Noirs made, in good seasons, in Alsace. Their lightness of body yet surprisingly powerful, fruity sweetness in scent and flavour echoes the classic method of cooking quail with grapes. Alsace Pinot Noir, often little darker than rose in colour, has little tannin and it can be served chilled. So can the other Pinot Noir alternatives that might be suggested – Sancerre *rosé* or red, or indeed wines made from the grape that in Beaujolais is frequently said to age like Pinot Noir, the Gamay. Light *dry* Beaujolais, such as Chiroubles or Côte-de-Brouilly, is therefore another red wine alternative which will be found suitable for quails.

If you prefer a white wine, Alsace Blanc has the right weight, fullness and spiciness of flavour; or other possibilities include Italian Pinot Grigio, New Zealand Sauvignon and Italian or Burgundian Chardonnay.

Hare

Hare is the meat with which to drink bargain hunters' under-rated strapping reds, especially those from the Rhone Valley appellations such as Vacqueyras, Gigondas, Cornas and Côte-Rotie, or from wine producing countries such as Italy and Portugal. Jugged hare is rightly served by the rumbustious rusticity of Cornas with its rich tangle of hedgerow berry and mushroom flavours, but roast saddle would be better suited by something more restrained and well-bred. At lightest this might be a Bourgogne Pinot Noir (basic red Burgundy). Other alternatives, in approximate ascending order of potency, include *gran reserva* Rioja, *riserva* Chianti, a full-blown Pomerol, or Portuguese *Garrafeira* (which is to say, specially selected Portuguese wine).

Wild duck

With wild duck look for quite large-scale red wines: instead of Côtes-du-Rhône Villages, for example, think in terms of Châteauneuf-du-Pape, and for the lighter recipes, in place of simple Beaujolais, substitute mature wine from the weightier of the Beaujolais *crus*, such as Morgon, Chénas or Moulin-à-Vent. Other wines that would be in the right ratio of weight and flavour would include Californian Cabernet Sauvignon and Pinot Noir, Australian Cabernet-Shiraz blends, Chilean Cabernet Sauvignon, or *bourgeois* and minor classed-growth clarets (red Bordeaux). It is not a bad principle, though, to adjust the weight of the wine to the size of the bird. For mallard Crozes-Hermitage could be good: with delicate teal it is best not to venture beyond St-Joseph, while in clarets the comparison might be that while mallard could take a powerful Pauillac, teal should not be tried beyond elegant Margaux. In Rioja, the full-bodied Rioja Alta *reservas* favour the mallard, the lighter, leaner and more delicate Alavesas the teal.

Partridge and pheasant

Partridge and pheasant would formerly certainly always have been accompanied with red Burgundy. The reasoning was sound. There is to mature Pinot Noir a decadent rotty sweetness that so much resembles the developing flavour of well-hung game that wines are actually described in vignerons' parlance as 'pheasanty' (*faisandée*). Take care, though. Red Burgundy is no longer as voluptuous as its reputation would have us believe it once was. Certainly these days highly celebrated and vastly expensive Burgundies can be thin, light, mean and disappointing compared to their peers from Bordeaux, and they seldom, if ever, pack the weight and punch of the big red Rhônes. The higher the game, the more flavoursome and characterful the wine required to cope with it, but in truth partridge or pheasant as eaten nowadays are unlikely to harm any well-flavoured dry red wine. Fine wines such as claret, top Chianti, Barbaresco, Barolo and Brunello di Montalcino from Italy or Rioja and Ribera del Duero wines from Spain have the right sense of occasion and splendour. The same can be said for 'boutique' wines from first-rate small wineries in California and Australia, whose excellent vintages will not be much less expensive than the European classics but may deliver even more impact. It is also worth trying, if you have the opportunity, Pinot Noir from the north-west Pacific states of America, Oregon and Washington. They are, as yet, the only New World Pinot Noirs which approach the best of Burgundy's vintages in quality. For light lunches of cold meat, patés and terrines, it is worth remembering that mature Beaujolais ages to resemble Pinot Noir from the neighbouring vineyards of Burgundy to the north. Light pheasant and partridge dishes are grand with *cru* Beaujolais from five to ten years old, as also with Italy's equivalents to Beaujolais – Dolcetto, Barbera or Valpolicella.

Venison

Venison is as fine as foil to good red Burgundy as can be found, but there are other possibilities; for example, the smoky, dusky, richly fruity and highly perfumed wines made from the Syrah grape of the northern Rhône. Penfold's Grange Hermitage, made from Shiraz, is Australia's greatest classic red, and would honour even the most noble venison haunch. Other possibilities include brambly and minty Californian Zinfandel, which can in the hands of top makers reach port-like standards of richness; and tarry and intense Italian Barolo or Brunello di Montalcino.

Slightly more rustic wines better suit venison stews: Cornas rather than Hermitage, and among the Italians, wines such as Ghemme, Spanna and Gattinara which, like Borolo, are made from the Nebbiolo grape though because they have less classic pedigree they tend to be rather cheaper.

Snipe, woodcock and grouse

With snipe, woodcock and grouse bring out red Burgundy. First rate Pinot Noir is the wine to accompany the greatest game birds. However, there are other options: the great and richly luscious clarets produced by the best Châteaux of Pomerol, such as Pétrus (which outprices even the most expensive red Burgundies), Trotanoy, or at rather lower prices Châteaux L'Enclos, de Sales, or Rouget. The best Barolas and Barbarescos of Italy, or wines such as Vega Sicilia, Protos and Pesquera from Spain, and Barca Velha from Portugal, would be proposed by champions of those countries' wines. Before risking them against snipe, woodcock or grouse, however, it would be wise to try them against some more easily secured game dish such as hare, venison or pheasant, to see how they suit your own personal taste.

White wine alternatives

As yet white wines have been mentioned only in relation to quail. There is a natural propensity to suppose that game must be accompanied by red wine. There are, however, great white wines which will go with game with success and with some recipes (for example, those involving cream sauces) white wines are more appropriate than red. Rabbit, being pale meat, is easily accompanied by white wine. Alsace Pinot Blanc or Franconian Bylvaner are especially appropriate and successful to drink with rabbit, though white Rioja, light Chardonnays such as Chablis, and dry white Graves would also be good. With wild duck recipes the exotically perfumed and spicily flavoured Alsace Gewürztraminer, with its scents of lychees and violets, can be deliciously appetizing, as also can German Riesling Auslese if it comes from a top grower and is not, like most German wines, over-sweetened.

For partridge and pheasant white wines of still greater substance are required: weightier and oak-aged Chardonnays such as good quality white Burgundy and premium label Chardonnays from Australia and California; top flight mature white Riojas; minor classed-growth Graves; and Hunter Valley Sémillon from Australia. For pheasant and partridge dishes German Riesling Auslese Trocken (dry) wines from top estates along the Rhine will also be found successful.

For the darker meats of pigeon, hare and venison only the sturdiest white wines will suffice. Matching the hierarchy to the game's league of status already described, suitable pairings would run: for pigeon, Chassagne– or Puligny-Montrachet (village white Burgundies); for hare, Chassagne– or

Puligny-Montrachet *premier cru*; and for venison *grand cru* such as Montrachet Bâtard-Montrachet, Bienvenues-Bâtard-Montrachet, Chevalier-Montrachet or Criots-Bâtard-Montrachet. Bear in mind that Chardonnay wines should never be too heavily chilled and the heavier, more unctuous and more alcoholic the wine, the more warming it will be for winter consumption and the less it should be cooled before serving.

The final choice

When determining one's final choice, the rules to bear in mind are those which apply to all food and wine selections. The weight, sweetness and acidity of the wine must be compatible with that found in the food, or the pairing will be a mis-match. Since game dishes are frequently accompanied with very flavoursome trimmings, which may be fruity, herby or vegetal in character, the accompaniments on the plate can be at least as important in determining the wine's suitability as the game itself. The wine must at least equal in intensity the concentration of flavour in the accoutrements if it is to make an equal match. It is also essential that strong flavours on the plate and in the glass should be readily compatible one with the other.

For Highland grouse garnished with raspberries, for example, a raspberryish red wine (young Pinot Noir or really first class *cru* Beaujolais such as Morgon Jean Descombes) will obviously suit best. Redcurrant jelly, on the other hand, suggests Cabernet Franc, a grape whose wines often have a distinctive redcurrent flavour; black-currant associates naturally with Cabernet Sauvignon, whose wines often resemble alcoholic Ribena; while the brambly wines which link to blackberry are pre-eminently Zinfandel and Syrah. Dolcetto and Valpolicella have an affinity with black cherries.

Dishes with a strong citric element in the sauce (such as those involving the Cumberland or Bigarade sauces) will require a wine with sufficient acidity. It is useful then to remember that Italian, Portuguese and southern Rhône red wines have extra acidity in their style, and among white wines Sauvignon and Riesling are outstanding for their appetizing acidity.

For cream sauces blander, more mellow, white wines are best: buttery Chardonnay and Tokay Pinot Gris being finest, and dry Muscat or Gewürztraminer interestingly aromatic and spicily flavoured alternatives.

Types of Game

Game refers to wild birds and animals which are hunted for sport as well as for food. The hunting, killing and selling of game is strictly controlled in Great Britain and the majority of game is protected by law, the exceptions being rabbits and woodpigeons.

There are certain times of the year when game cannot be shot and these 'seasons' vary slightly according to the nesting and mating patterns of the individual species. Outside of the season, not only is it illegal to kill game but it is also an offence to sell game: unless it has been imported into the country when already dead. Only licensed butchers and poulterers are allowed to deal in game and it can be offered for sale up to ten days after the end of the season. The restrictions on the sale of home-reared game apply to frozen animals as well as to fresh ones. However, there are companies that specialise in importing game for out-of-season sale. Some game, notably venison, is now farmed. Certain birds must not be killed and these include wild geese, Garganey teal, Long-tailed duck and Scaup duck.

A note of the season for each type of game is given in the following pages, along with advice on identifying birds and the best cooking methods to use. In the section which follows, the details of preparing and cooking game are outlined; however you will find that game is readily available dressed for the oven, not only from specialist butchers but also from good supermarkets where it is often sold frozen.

Capercaillie

Season: October 1st to January 31st.

The capercaillie is a member of the grouse family, originating from Scandinavia. It is found today in small numbers in the northern areas of Scotland where it has been re-introduced following previous extinction from this country. It is not a common game bird but when available it should be treated in the same way as grouse, and grouse can be substituted for it in recipes. This is a large bird which can weigh up to 4 kg/9 lb and it should be hung for about 3–4 days, depending on conditions and personal preference.

Grouse

Season: August 12th to December 10th.

There are several different members of the grouse family as well as the capercaillie, including the blackcock (also known as the heathpoult or black grouse) and the ptarmigan which comes from Europe and North America. However, the smaller Scottish grouse or red grouse (weighing about 675 g/1½ lb each) is considered to be the finest for flavour.

Young grouse shot early in the season are the most tender and they can be slightly tough at the beginning of December, just before the season ends. Look for birds with pointed flight feathers and soft pliable feet, also a downy breast. Hang for about 3–4 days, depending on conditions and preference. The young birds are ideal for roasting or grilling and the older ones can be casseroled. An average-sized grouse serves one or two.

Partridge

Season: September 1st to February 1st.

This bird is related to the pheasant and there are two main varieties of partridge: the grey partridge which is the most common and considered to be the better bird and the red-legged, or French, partridge. When selecting birds, look for pliable, yellow-brown feet as they turn grey when the bird is older. The flight feathers should have pointed tips and the under feathers should be rounded, the beak of a young bird is fairly sharp. The best birds are obtained in October and November.

As a guide, partridges should be hung for about a week. Young birds can be roasted, older ones should be casseroled. It is usual to serve one partridge per person or one bird can be split before cooking to serve two. The average weight for a partridge is 350–400 g/12–14 oz.

Pheasant

Season: October 1st to February 1st.

The pheasant is probably the best known and most easily obtainable of the game birds. Pheasants are sold dressed, ready for the oven, or they can be purchased in the traditional brace, consisting of a male and female bird. The male bird is easily distinguished by its bright plumage but the hen pheasant is rather dull by comparison, with pale brown feathers. However, the hen pheasant is the most tender and has the best flavour whereas the cock pheasant can be rather dry and slightly tough.

When looking for a bird, notice the feet which should be fairly smooth when the bird is young and tend to become scaly in appearance as the pheasant ages. The breast of a young bird should still be downy. Pheasants can be hung for some time, anything from a few days to two weeks, but this is a matter of taste and a source of great controversy among gourmets and cooks alike. The best months for buying pheasant are November and December.

The younger birds or tender hen pheasants can be roasted but if they are older or likely to be tough, then they should be braised or casseroled. An average weight for pheasant is about 1.5 kg/3 lb and the hen is smaller than the cock. A smaller bird will serve three, or the larger one can be made to serve four, depending on the way in which it is prepared and served.

Pigeon

Season: Available all year.

There are two types of pigeon: the woodpigeon which is larger and has dark flesh and the stronger flavour, and the tame pigeon which has pale flesh and resembles young chicken more than game. The average weight for a pigeon is just over 450 g/1 lb and they are best from August to October. Look for birds with pink legs as they tend to be younger. Pigeons are best cooked by moist methods, braised or casseroled or in pies.

Quail

Season: Available all the year.

Quail are protected by law in Britain and are not shot in the wild; however, they are farmed and are therefore available all year round, both fresh and frozen. They are very small birds, weighing about 150 g/5 oz, and are often sold as well as being served in pairs.

They are tender and delicate in flavour and much esteemed by gourmets. Suitable for grilling or roasting, quails are not hung and they are usually cooked whole, without being drawn.

Snipe

Season: August 12th to January 31st.

Small birds, not widely available in shops, and best killed when plump in November. Related to the woodcock, snipe live only in marshy land.

Weighing about 100 g/4 oz each, snipe are considered a delicacy cooked whole, trussed with their long, pointed beaks skewered through their legs. Hang the birds for a few days, or up to a week. The gizzard can be removed before roasting or grilling. Serve one snipe per person.

Wild Duck

Season: September 1st to January 31st.

There are many varieties of wild duck but the mallard is the most common and it is also the largest. Other common varieties include the pintail, teal

and widgeon; the teal being the smallest. The best months for wild duck are November and December and they should be eaten fresh, without hanging. A mallard will serve two to three; the teal serves one.

Woodcock

Season: October 1st to January 31st.

A relative of the snipe, the woodcock is found in woodland as well as marshy land. Rarely available in the shops, this bird is prized for its flavour. Weighing about 150 g/5 oz serve one snipe per person. Hang these birds for up to a week, then cook them by roasting or braising.

Opposite, back to front: *capercaillie, partridge, snipe and woodcock (right); hanging, left to right: grouse, hen and cock pheasants.* Below, hanging left to right: *hare, rabbit and mallard; lying, back to front: widgeon, pigeon and quail (left).*

Venison

Season: England and Wales
Red deer, stags: August 1st to April 30th.
  hinds: November 1st to February 28/29th.
Fallow deer, bucks: August 1st to April 30th.
  does: November 1st to April 30th.
Roe deer, bucks: April 1st to September 30th.
  does: November 1st to February 28/29th.

Scotland
Red deer, stags: July 1st to October 20th.
  hinds: October 21st to February 15th.
Fallow deer, bucks: August 1st to April 30th.
  does: October 21st to February 15th.
Roe deer, bucks: April 1st to October 20th.
  does: October 21st to March 31st.

The red deer is the largest and most splendid-looking beast; the meat of the roe deer is paler and the least gamey; and the fallow deer is considered to have the best flavour. The meat of any type should be fine-grained and dark, with firm white fat. Young animals or fawns up to 18 months old produce delicate meat which should not be marinated before cooking. The meat of the male is preferred to that of the female and older venison is usually marinated, larded or barded before cooking as it is dry.

Venison is always hung, otherwise it would have little flavour. The whole carcass is hung for 10–14 days, depending on the weather and the strength of flavour required. Small cuts need hanging for about a week; however, if you buy the meat from a butcher, then it will have been hung in advance. If you prefer well-hung venison, then do ask your butcher if he suggests that the meat ought to be hung for a while before cooking.

If you do have fresh venison, then inspect the meat thoroughly before hanging it. If there is any musty smell, the meat should be washed in lukewarm water and dried thoroughly. Rub the meat with a mixture of ground ginger and black pepper, then hang it in a cool, dry, well-ventilated place. Check the venison daily and wipe off any moisture. To test if the meat is ready, run a sharp knife into the flesh near the bone. If it smells very strong, cook the meat at once or wash it with warm milk and water, then dry it and cover it with plenty of ginger and pepper. Wash the spices off before cooking. Haunch, saddle and loin are the prime cuts for roasting, or they can be cut into cutlets or steaks for grilling. Shoulder is a fairly tender cut which can be roasted or braised. The neck and other pieces of meat are stewed or they can be minced or made into sausages. The fat should always be removed from venison before cooking as it has an unpleasant flavour.

Hare

Two types of hare are fairly common in Britain, the English or brown hare and the Scottish or blue hare; the brown hare is considered to have the best flavour. An animal under a year old is known as a leveret, distinguished by a small bony knot near the foot, a short neck, long joints, smooth sharp claws, a narrow cleft in its lip and soft ears.

Hare should be hung, whole, for 7–10 days, depending on the weather. It should hang from the back legs in a cool, dry, well-ventilated place. Catch its blood in a dish. Add one or two drops of vinegar to the blood to prevent clotting; store, covered, in the refrigerator.

The back, saddle and the hind legs can be roasted; the shoulders or forelegs are better cooked by braising or casseroling, or they can be jugged.

Rabbit

Wild and tame rabbit are closely related but the difference in flavour is derived from the diet and habitat.

The meat of wild rabbit is darker and it has a more gamey flavour. A freshly killed rabbit is treated in the same way as hare but it must be paunched (gutted) immediately it is killed and there is no need to hang the animal for any length of time. Although the skin of the rabbit is usually left on once it is paunched, there is opinion which suggests that by skinning the animal immediately the meat will not have the slightly musty taste which is often associated with it.

Three to four month old rabbit is best, with thick foot joints, smooth claws, a flexible jaw and soft ears. The eyes should be bright, the fat whitish and the liver bright red. Average weight 2–2.25 kg/4½–5 lb but can be up to 4 kg/9 lb.

Preparing and Cooking Game

All water birds should be eaten as fresh as possible but most other game birds of any size should be hung before being eaten. This process serves two purposes: to tenderise the meat and to give the characteristic gamey flavour. The birds should be hung in a cool place where air can circulate freely. The hanging time depends on the weather, the type of bird and individual taste. Birds which are considered to be over-hung for most tastes have a distinct greenish or blueish tinge to the skin. In this case they should be washed with salted water which contains a little vinegar, then rinsed.

Plucking

The first stage in the preparation of game, once it has been hung, is to pluck out all feathers and down, away from the direction of growth. Ducks should be plucked as soon as possible after they are killed, preferably while still warm. To avoid unnecessary mess, pluck birds in a draught-free place, preferably a shed or outhouse.

1 Extend one wing and pull out the under feathers. Work down towards the breast, leaving the feathers on the very tips of the wings. Repeat with the other wing, turning the bird over to pluck the other side of each wing. Pull off the feathers on the back, leaving just the tail feathers. Snap off the large feathers at the ends of the wings.

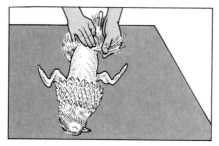

2 Next pluck the breast of the bird, holding the skin to keep it taut. Again pull out just a few feathers at a time and work down from the head towards the tail.

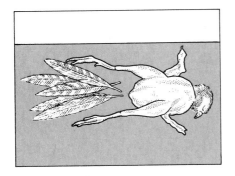

3 Pluck the legs and the lower half of the neck. The head and top part of the neck will be cut off (except in the case of snipe if the bird is to be skewered on its beak). Remove the tail feathers.

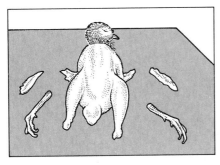

4 Cut off the wing tips at the joint and cut off the feet, or trim them if you want to leave them on for cooking.

5 Cut off the head about halfway along the neck. Cut a ring round the outer skin, then pull or cut off the head, leaving the skin neatly severed.

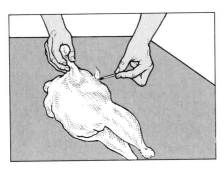

6 Singe the bird all over to remove any trace of down. Do this by passing the bird over a gas flame, or use matches. Long matches are best; light the match and let the smoke burn away, then move it over the bird, just above the skin.

Drawing

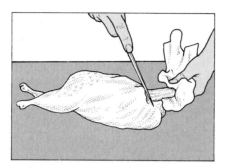

1 Hold the neck with a clean dry cloth, pull the skin back from it to leave it bare. At the base of the neck cut through the meat only.

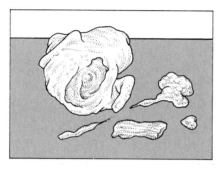

2 Still using the cloth to hold the neck, twist it round to break the bone. Cut through the bone to neaten the end, then draw the neck out from the skin and set it aside. It can be used to make stock.

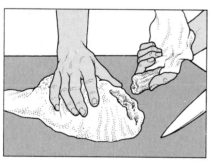

3 Push one finger inside the neck cavity to loosen the wind pipe. Pull away the wind pipe and the gullet. Remove the crop – a small pouch filled with food which has not travelled further into the bird. Discard the crop.

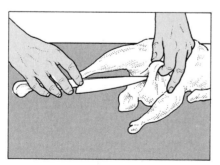

4 Make a small slit above the vent, between it and the tail. Do not cut too far into the bird as the intestines should not be cut.

5 At the neck end loosen the gizzard (the bird's second stomach) with one finger so that it will pull away easily. Use one or two fingers of your other hand and insert them into the slit at the vent of the bird. Gently feel inside the cavity and loosen the contents, then draw out all the intestines and the gizzard – they should come out fairly cleanly and all in one piece.

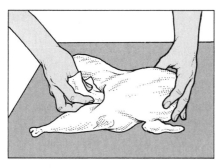

6 Wipe the inside of the bird with absorbent kitchen paper, then rinse it out thoroughly with plenty of running water. Smaller birds need less rinsing and they should be handled carefully to avoid damaging them.

7 Separate the liver from the gall bladder, taking care not to split the bladder as it has a strong, bitter flavour that will spoil the flesh of the bird if it comes in contact with it. Split the gizzard and rinse it out to remove all grit. The liver, gizzard, neck and heart are the giblets and they can be used to make stock.

MRS BEETON'S TIP

Larger birds can be boned out in the same way as poultry and the butcher will do this. If you bone the bird, then use a small, sharp, pointed knife. Cut along the back of the bird, then work on one side, sliding the knife between the bones and the flesh. Work down to the joints and ease all the meat off them. Leave the meat attached at the breast bone and work on the second side in the same way. When the meat is all free, carefully cut it off the breast bone, taking the smallest sliver of bone. For success, avoid breaking through the skin of the bird.

Trussing

Birds are trussed to keep them in a neat shape while they are cooking and to secure any stuffing. The easiest way to truss a bird is with a large needle and strong thread or fine string. Special, long, thick trussing needles are available from cook's shops. There are several ways of trussing birds, using one or two pieces of string inserted through the thighs, then wrapped back around the wings. Tying the legs neatly in place is adequate trussing for small game birds. If one piece is used, longer ends must be left and the string taken from the legs around the wings, then back to the legs.

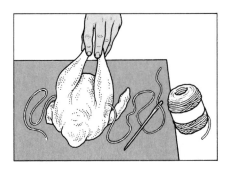

1 Put the bird on its back and hold the legs together forming a 'V' shape pointing towards the neck end. Insert the trussing needle into one leg, then push it through the body and out through the other leg. The string should pass through just above the thigh bone. Leave good lengths of string to tie the legs firmly in place.

2 Tie the leg ends neatly, then re-thread the needle and thread it through the wings. Leave a long end of string and secure the flap of skin at the wing end of the bird to keep it neatly in place.

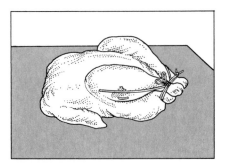

3 Take the string round underneath the body and towards the leg end of the bird. Tie off the ends to keep the whole body in a neat, secure shape.

Barding

Barding is the term used for wrapping or covering the birds (or a joint) with pieces of fat. This prevents the breast meat from drying out during cooking and it is used for birds which have dry meat, containing little fat. Pork fat, from the belly, is usually used. Alternatively use fatty streaky bacon.

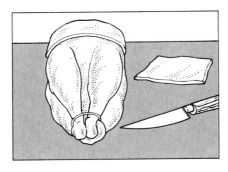

1 For barding cut thin, even and neat slices of fat from belly of pork. The bird should be ready trussed. Lay the fat over the breast side of the bird, using as many slices as necessary to cover the breast completely.

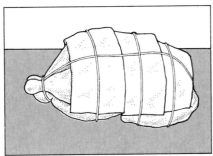

2 Tie the fat neatly in place. The bird is now ready for cooking: the fat should be removed shortly before the end of the cooking time so as to brown the skin.

Roasting Times for Game Birds

The following times are a guide for roasting unstuffed birds. For a small stuffed bird up to 375g/13oz in weight allow up to 10 minutes extra; for a larger stuffed bird allow between 15–18 minutes extra cooking time.

Blackcock 40–50 minutes
Grouse 25–30 minutes
Pheasant 45–60 minutes
Partridge 20–30 minutes
Teal 15–20 minutes
Widgeon 25–30 minutes

Pintail 20–30 minutes
Mallard 30–45 minutes
Tame pigeon 30–40 minutes
Squab 15–25 minutes
Woodpigeon 35–45 minutes
Other small birds 10–15 minutes

Skinning Rabbit or Hare

Rabbits are paunched or drawn before they are skinned and they are not hung. Hares are hung and skinned before they are drawn. The method of skinning is the same for both animals and this is a task which you can expect the butcher to complete if the animal is purchased. In fact, both paunching and skinning are only carried out at home if a freshly killed animal is obtained. This is not to be recommended to those who are squeamish. The process is not as messy as paunching the animal but you should equip yourself with a sharp, pointed knife, and a pair of kitchen scissors are useful.

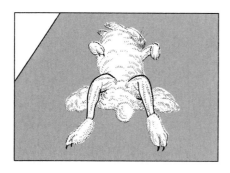

1 Start with the hind legs of the animal. Lay it on its back and slit the skin down each leg, then pull it off so that it hangs down towards the back of the animal.

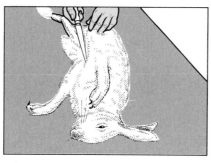

2 Cut the skin down the length of the belly of the animal, from the slits made down the back legs. A rabbit will already have been paunched but take care not to split the belly of a hare.

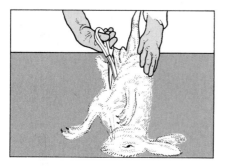

3 Loosen the skin from the meat on either side of the slit, then ease it away from the flesh, up towards the spine on both sides, until the centre of the body is completely free from its skin.

4 Turn the animal over and hold the hind legs firmly with one hand, then carefully pull the skin off the back of the animal to leave the rear end skinned.

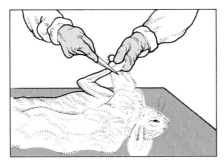

5 To remove the skin from the fore legs, carefully cut round it just above both paws. Peel the skin off each leg, using the point of a knife to ease it off like sleeves.

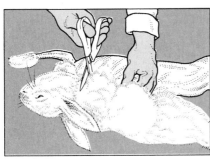

6 Ease the skin off the neck, then carefully cut it free all round below the head. The head can be chopped off at this stage.

Note: For a traditional roast the head is skinned and the ears are left with their fur. Skinning the head is difficult and it is best to ask the butcher to do this if you want to roast it on the animal. The skin has to be cut around the eyes, mouth and round the base of the ears but it should be left attached to the body skin. It can be peeled off from the body end. If you do this, have a small, sharp, pointed knife at the ready and use the point to carefully ease the skin off the head as you pull it free.

Alternatively, the head can be left with its fur on, in which case it should be covered with cooking foil during roasting. The most acceptable method is to chop off the head before cooking.

Paunching Hare or Rabbit

Paunching is the term used for gutting a rabbit or hare. Rabbits are paunched when they are freshly killed but hares are hung whole. Any blood that drips out of the hare as it hangs should be collected and chilled but blood also collects inside the animal, in the chest. Before paunching the hare have a basin ready to catch the blood when you split the chest. The blood is used to thicken the sauce of jugged hare. Protect the work surface with newspaper and lay clean greaseproof paper on top. When finished, thoroughly rinse the animal.

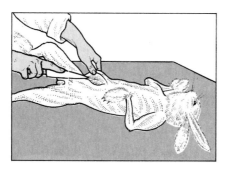

1 Using a sharp knife, slit the hare down its belly towards the rear end. Do not cut in too far as you may slit the intestines.

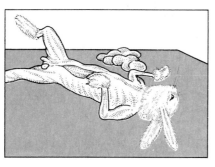

2 Open out the slit and ease your fingers round the intestines to loosen them. Pull the innards out, leaving the kidneys in place. They should come out roughly in one piece.

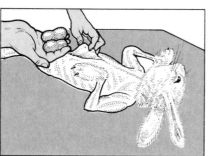

3 The liver is higher up near the rib cage. Gently pull it out with your fingers. Rinse the liver in cold water, pat it dry and use it in stuffings or sauces.

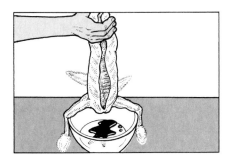

4 Have ready a bowl to catch the blood and tilt the animal so that the head end is downwards. Cut down into the chest where the blood will have collected during hanging, then tip it into a bowl.

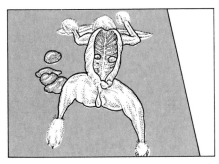

5 Remove the heart. Cut the gall bladder off the liver, taking care not to split it, then discard the bladder. Reserve the heart and lungs, the kidneys are left in place if the hare is to be roasted. The liver and heart can be chopped and used for a stuffing.

Trussing Hare or Rabbit

The simplest method of trussing is to cut off the head and neck, leaving a flap of skin which can be skewered over the cut surface like the skin over the neck end of a chicken. The front and back legs are tied together, or skewered to keep them neatly in place under the body. If the head is left on, cover the ears with foil. If it is not skinned, remove the eyes and cover the head with foil.

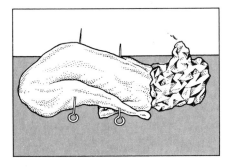

1 A trussed hare with the unskinned head left on and covered with foil.

Jointing Hare or Rabbit

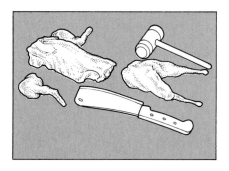

1 *The head should be removed. Cut off each foreleg in one piece. Cut off the hind legs where they join on to the back (or saddle) of the animal. First cut straight across. You will need a heavy cook's knife and a mallet or rolling pin to tap the knife through the bones.*

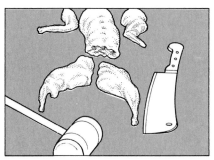

2 *Cut between the hind legs to make two separate joints. The hind legs of rabbit are usually left whole unless they are to be used in a pie in which case they can be cut into two portions.*

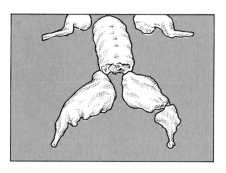

3 *The hind legs of a hare should be split into thigh portions and lower leg portions, cutting through at the joint, again tapping the knife through the bones if necessary.*

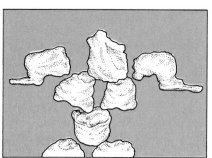

4 *Separate the rib cage from the saddle, cutting through the spine as before, about a third of the way down the back. Cut the saddle across to give two joints. The front joint from the saddle can be chopped in half lengthways to split it into two joints.*

Carving Hare or Rabbit

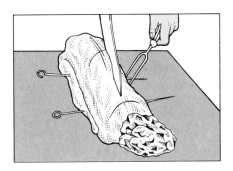

1 Carve the hare before arranging it on a plate for serving. Make short cuts across the spine in two or three places, then cut through down the length of the spine, from head to tail.

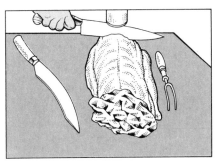

2 Cut across the spine towards the hindquarters, then cut between the legs to make two serving portions. This releases any stuffing in the body cavity and it can be scooped out at this stage.

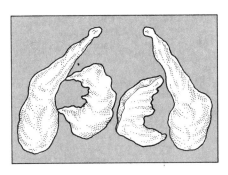

3 Divide the thigh and lower leg from the body meat to cut each of the two hind portions into two separate pieces.

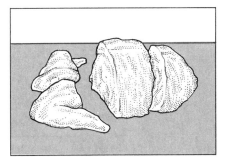

4 Cut across the spine just behind the shoulders to separate the saddle from the fore quarters. The saddle can be cut across into two or three portions. Cut off the head and cut fore legs into two further portions if preferred.

Larding Venison

Larding is the term used for threading strips of fat through meat before cooking. The fat is cut from belly of pork in neat slices, then the slices are cut into strips. A special larding needle is available, with a grip to hold a strip of fat at one end. Larding is used for very lean cuts of meat that tend to become dry on cooking. The strips of fat moisten the meat as it cooks.

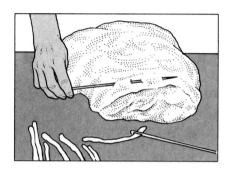

1 Cut neat strips of fat: they do not have to be too long but they should be fairly even in thickness. Larding is made easier if a fine skewer is first used to pierce the meat, this helps to prevent the fat from breaking as you pull it through with the larding needle. Pierce the meat as though sewing running stitches, inserting a fine skewer, then pushing it out about 2.5–5cm/1–2 inches along.

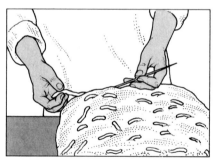

2 Put a piece of fat in the larding needle, then thread it through the meat, following the line cut by the skewer. Leave a short piece of fat protruding at each end of the stitch, then continue to lard the piece of meat all over, keeping the spaces between the fat even.

MRS BEETON'S TIP

The process of larding meat is not a difficult one but it is time consuming. The fat should be evenly cut into narrow strips measuring about 5 mm/¼ inch wide and up to 5 cm/2 inches long. Larding bacon is specially prepared without saltpetre but pork fat can be used. Pierce and lard a small area at a time, working in a methodical pattern over the joint.

Preparing a Haunch of Venison for Cooking

A haunch of venison can be boned out completely, then tied neatly in place before cooking. The butcher will usually do this for you but should you want to attempt the task yourself it is not very difficult but it is time consuming. You will need a very sharp pointed knife and you should start from the wide end, cutting the meat off the bone. Work very closely to the bone, easing the meat away with your fingers. Alternatively, split the haunch down one side, then cut out the bone.

1 If the butcher has not already done so, chop off the bone end close to the meat and pull away any tendons. Trim all fat off the meat, cutting it away thinly using a sharp knife.

2 Once the meat is trimmed it should be larded, then marinated. Place the joint in a suitable dish, one which is large enough to hold the venison and deep enough to hold the marinade. A large gratin dish, lasagne dish or similar is ideal. During marinating the meat should be turned frequently and basted.

MRS BEETON'S TIP

Dry meats are marinated before they are roasted to moisten them. The marinade imparts the flavour of the chosen ingredients to the meat and, where necessary, it can help to tenderise the joint. Rich marinades can be used with venison and they can include red wine, spices and fresh herbs. Juniper berries, mace and cinnamon are all suitable spices. Bay leaves, parsely, thyme or rosemary can be used. Since the meat lacks fat, oil can be added – olive, walnut or hazelnut oils also flavour the meat.

Carving a Saddle of Venison

The easiest way to prepare and serve saddle of venison is to ask the butcher for a boned and rolled joint which will include the tender fillet. Boned and rolled joints can be obtained in a variety of sizes, to cater for individual requirements. However, joints on the bone tend to be far larger and they may have the fillets left on. The fillets should be cut off in one piece and sliced. A rolled joint can be cut across into thick slices. The following steps are a guide to the more difficult process of carving the whole, unboned, saddle joint.

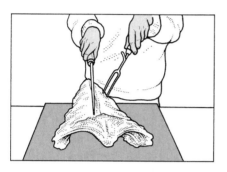

1 First carve the meat off the top, or loin, of the saddle. Starting in the middle to one side of the bone, cut downwards as near to the bone as possible.

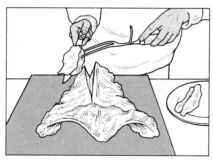

2 The next cut should be at a slight angle but down to meet the base of the first cut and release the first slice of meat.

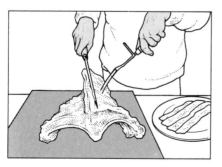

3 When one slice has been removed the carving is simplified and the rest of the same side of the haunch should be carved in neat, long slices. Carve the opposite side in the same way.

4 *If the fillets were not removed before cooking, remove each in one piece: to do this first slice down as near to the bone as possible, then cut outwards from the base to remove the fillet in one piece. Remove the fillet from the second side in the same way.*

5 *Cut the fillets into neat slices and serve them with the long slices taken from the top of the saddle.*

Carving a Haunch of Venison

A haunch of venison on the bone is not as difficult to carve as a saddle joint. The meat is taken off the sides, working on both sides of the joint to cut away large, even slices. The remaining small pieces of meat can be sliced off in small pieces but these are not prime portions. A boned haunch can be cut across into slices. Unlike beef, when carving venison the meat should be cut into fairly thick slices.

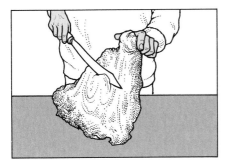

1 *Holding the joint firmly by the bone end, cut neat slices off one side, then turn the leg slightly to carve the meat off the other side. The remaining meat can be cut off in small slices.*

Carving Roast Pheasant

1 Remove the legs by cutting between the breast and the point where the legs join the body. The bones should be cleanly cut and a pair of stout kitchen scissors may be useful. The legs can be cut into two portions, the thigh and the lower leg, although they are best left whole.

2 Next the wings should be removed, cutting them off close to the body and again using a pair of kitchen scissors to snip through awkward bones.

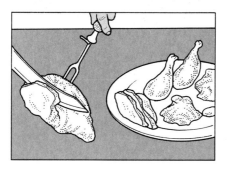

3 Lastly the breast meat should be carved off, first one side then the other. Cut the meat into neat, even slices, as thinly as possible.

SOUPS

All-purpose Stock

450g/1lb onions, carrots, celery and leeks, sliced
1kg/2lb cooked or raw bones, raw meat trimmings, giblets and bacon rinds
salt • 1 bay leaf • 4 black peppercorns

Retain a piece of onion skin for a brown stock. Put the bones and meat trimmings into a saucepan. Cover with cold water and add 1.25ml/½ tsp salt for each 1.1 litres/2 pints water used. Heat slowly to simmering point. Add the other ingredients. Simmer, uncovered, for at least 3 hours. Strain and cool quickly by standing the pan in chilled water. When cold, skim off the fat. Use as required.

MAKES ABOUT 1 LITRE/2 PINTS

Game Stock

carcass of 1 game bird, including the giblets, for example pheasant or grouse
cleaned feet of bird (optional)
5ml/1tsp salt
1 onion, sliced
1 celery stick, sliced
4 white peppercorns
1 bouquet garni

Break or chop the carcass into manageable pieces. Put the carcass, giblets, and feet, if used, in a large saucepan. Cover with cold water and add the salt. Heat to boiling point. Draw the pan off the heat and leave to stand for 2–3 minutes, then skim off any fat. Add the vegetables, peppercorns and bouquet garni. Simmer very gently for 3–4 hours. Strain, cool and skim.

MAKES ABOUT 1 LITRE/2 PINTS

Game Soup

meaty remains of 1 roast pheasant or 2 – 3 smaller game birds
50g/2oz lean rindless bacon
25g/1oz butter or margarine
1 litre/2 pints Game Stock (opposite)
1 onion, sliced
1 large carrot, sliced
1 bouquet garni
1 blade of mace
1 chicken's liver or 50g/2oz calf's liver
25g/1oz flour
15 – 30ml/2 – 3tbsp port or sherry (optional)
salt and pepper

Cut any large pieces of meat from the carcass of the game birds and cut the bacon into small cubes. Melt the fat in a frying pan and fry the game pieces and bacon lightly. Put to one side.

Put the stock and game bones in a large, heavy saucepan and add the vegetables, bouquet garni and mace. Heat to boiling point, cover and simmer for 2–2½ hours.

Remove any skin and tubes from the liver; add the liver to the soup pan and simmer for another 15 minutes. Lift out the liver, then strain the soup through a sieve or colander into a clean pan. Discard the bones. Pureé the liver and reserved meat and bacon with a little of the fat set aside from cooking the bacon if a rich purée is wanted. Reheat the rest of the fat in the pan, stir in the flour and cook for 4–5 minutes, stirring all the time until nut brown. Stir this roux gradually into the meat purée.

Heat the soup to boiling point, then draw the pan off the heat. Stir in the pureé mixture in small spoonfuls. Return to a gentle heat and stir until the soup thickens to the preferred consistency. Add the port or sherry, if used, and season to taste.

Serve with fried bread croûtons or sprigs of watercress.

SERVES 4

Cream of Pheasant and Lentil Soup

meaty remains of 1 roast pheasant
50g/2oz rindless bacon
25g/1oz butter or margarine
1 litre/2 pints Game Stock (page 40)
1 onion, chopped
1 leek, sliced
1 bouquet garni
1 blade of mace
100g/4oz red lentils
salt and pepper
150ml/¼ pint single cream
blanched rings of leek to garnish (optional)

Remove any large pieces of meat from the pheasant carcass and cut the bacon into small cubes. Melt the butter or margarine in a frying pan and fry the game pieces and bacon. Remove and keep to one side. Put the stock and game bones in a large saucepan or flameproof casserole and add the onion, leek, bouquet garni and mace. Bring to the boil, then cover and simmer for 2 hours.

Strain the soup and put into a clean pan. Discard the bones. Add the lentils to the soup and cook for 1 hour or until they are fallen. Strain the lentils from the soup and place with the reserved meat and bacon, then purée the mixture. Removing the soup from the heat, add a spoonful of the purée at a time to the soup. Once all the purée has been added, reheat to boiling point and season to taste. Remove from the heat, stir in the cream and garnish the soup with a few rings of blanched leek, if liked. Serve immediately, before the soup cools.

S E R V E S   4

MRS BEETON'S TIP

Blanching is the term used for plunging food into rapidly boiling water, cooking it very briefly, then draining and cooling it in iced water.

Top: Cream of Pheasant and Lentil Soup; Below: Old English Hare Soup (page 44)

Old English Hare Soup

Illustrated on previous page

This soup can be served with Forcemeat Balls (page 172), in which case it makes a satisfying lunch or supper when served with crusty bread.

1 hare, prepared and paunched
1.5 litres/2½ pints All-purpose Stock (page 40) or water
30ml/2tbsp dripping or lard
1 onion, sliced
1 large carrot, sliced
½ turnip, diced
1 small parsnip, sliced
1 celery stick, sliced
1 bouquet garni
5ml/1tsp salt
8 black peppercorns
15ml/1tbsp flour
30 – 45ml/2 – 3tbsp port

Cut the meat off the back and legs of the hare, and use for another recipe. Only the head, flaps, bones and blood of the hare are used for the soup.

Split the head, break the bones and put them and the meat trimmings into a large saucepan. Cover with stock or water, and stand for 1 hour.

Heat the fat in a saucepan, add the vegetables and fry until golden-brown. Lift out the vegetables and reserve the fat in the pan. Heat the bones and liquid very slowly to simmering point. Add the fried vegetables, bouquet garni, salt and peppercorns. Simmer for 3–4 hours.

Meanwhile, add the flour to the fat in the saucepan and fry gently, until golden-brown, stirring all the time. Strain the soup. Remove all pieces of meat from the bones and cut them into small dice. Whisk the fried flour into the soup and heat to boiling point, whisking all the time. Stir in the meat, blood and port. Check the seasoning and reheat without boiling.

SERVES 6

Game Soup with Chestnuts

This is an excellent, seasonal soup which is ideal for serving during Christmas week, either as a first course or as a warming lunch.

meaty remains of 1 roast pheasant or 2 – 3 smaller game birds
50g/2oz lean rindless bacon
25g/1oz butter or margarine
450g/1lb chestnuts
1 litre/2 pints Game Stock (page 40)
1 onion, sliced • 1 large carrot, sliced
1 bouquet garni • 1 blade of mace
25g/1oz flour
15ml/1tbsp port or sherry (optional)
salt and pepper

Cut any large pieces of meat from the carcass of the game birds and cut the bacon into small cubes. Melt the fat in a frying pan and fry the game pieces and bacon lightly. Put to one side while preparing the chestnuts.

Score the chestnuts on the rounded side of their shells, then boil them for 15 minutes. Drain, cool slightly and remove the shells and skins. Place the stock and game bones in a large, heavy saucepan or flameproof casserole and add the vegetables and chestnuts. Put in the bouquet garni and mace, then heat to boiling point; cover and simmer for 2–2½ hours.

Strain the soup into a clean pan, discarding the bones. Purée the meat, bacon and chestnuts with a little fat from the pan to obtain a rich purée. Reheat the remaining fat in the saucepan or casserole, stir in the flour and cook for 4–5 minutes, stirring all the time, until nut brown. Stir this roux gradually into the meat purée. Heat the soup to boiling point, then remove from the heat. Stir in the purée mixture in small spoonfuls. Return the soup to a gentle heat and stir until the soup thickens to the required consistency. Add the port or sherry, if used, and season to taste.

S E R V E S   4

Rabbit and Bacon Soup

1 rabbit
100g/4oz lean bacon or *pickled pork*
2 litres/4 pints water or *All-purpose Stock (page 40)*
1 bouquet garni
1 bay leaf
1 blade of mace
2 cloves
2 onions
1 small turnip, finely diced
2 celery sticks, finely diced
60ml/4tbsp flour
150ml/¼ pint milk or *half milk and half cream*
salt and pepper
5ml/1tsp lemon juice

Prepare and joint the rabbit. Blanch it by covering it with cold water in a saucepan and heating to boiling point. Drain and rinse. Put the rabbit and whole piece of bacon or pork in a large saucepan. Cover with the water or stock. Add the bouquet garni, bay leaf and mace. Heat to boiling point, cover and simmer very gently for 1 hour.

Press a clove in each onion. Add the vegetables to the soup, cover and simmer for a further 1½ hours. Strain the soup. Remove and dice some meat from the bones. (The rest of the rabbit meat can be used for a fricassée or similar dish.) Dice the bacon or pork. Add the diced meat to the soup. Blend the flour with the milk, or milk and cream, and stir it into the soup. Heat until the soup is thickened, stirring all the time. (If cream is used, add it to the hot soup off the heat and serve at once.) Season to taste and sharpen the soup with the lemon juice.

SERVES 6 TO 8

MRS BEETON'S TIP

Liver, kidneys and heart of rabbit have a strong flavour and so can be used or left out, as preferred.

ROASTS, GRILLS
AND FRIED GAME

Pheasant with Ham and Mushroom Stuffing

Illustrated on page 50

Wild mushrooms, tossed in butter, are good with this dish.

2 pheasants
½ onion • 50g/2oz butter

STUFFING
25g/1oz butter or margarine
100g/4oz finely chopped onion
100g/4oz mushrooms, chopped
50g/2oz ham, chopped
75g/3oz soft white breadcrumbs
salt and pepper
15ml/1tbsp Game Stock (page 40) (optional)

GARNISH
watercress sprigs

Wash the pheasant giblets and cover with cold water. Add the half onion and simmer gently for 40 minutes to make stock for the gravy.

Make the stuffing. Melt the butter or maragarine and cook the onion until soft. Add the mushrooms to the onion; cook for a few minutes. Add the ham and breadcrumbs. Stir, add salt and pepper and the stock if the stuffing is too crumbly.

Set the oven at 375°F/190°C/gas 5. Divide the stuffing between the birds, filling the body cavities only. Truss the birds neatly and put in a roasting tin; spread with the butter. Roast for 45 – 60 minutes, depending on the size of the birds. Baste occasionally while roasting. Transfer the birds to a heated serving dish and remove the trussing strings. Garnish with watercress and serve with gravy made from the giblet stock.

SERVES 6

Salmis of Pheasant

Illustrated overleaf

Salmis is the term used for a dish which includes two cooking methods; the
first is roasting, the second braising or stewing in a rich brown sauce,
usually with the addition of wine. This is a popular, and traditional,
method for cooking game.

50g/2oz butter
1 pheasant
2.5ml/½ tsp grated lemon rind
2 shallots, chopped
1.25ml/¼ tsp dried thyme
1 bay leaf
300ml/½ pint Foundation Brown Sauce (page 160)
about 150ml/¼ pint Madeira (optional)
salt and pepper
6 – 8 button mushrooms,
croûtons of fried bread to garnish (optional)

Set the oven at 400°F/200°C/gas 6. Melt the butter in a roasting tin. Baste
the bird well with the hot butter and roast it on a rack for 40–45 minutes,
basting frequently. When cooked, pour the butter used for basting into a
saucepan and add the lemon rind. Add the shallots with the thyme and bay
leaf. Remove from the heat, joint and bone the bird, put the flesh on one
side. Add the bones to the saucepan and fry well. Drain off and reserve any
excess butter. Add the Brown Sauce and the wine, if used, to the bones.
Season to taste and simmer for 10 minutes. Strain the sauce, add the meat
and simmer for 20 minutes.

Reheat the reserved butter and fry the mushrooms in it. Check the
seasoning. Serve the pheasant with the mushrooms on top and add a
garnish of croûtons, if liked.

SERVES 4

Top: Salmis of Pheasant (previous page); Below: Pheasant with Ham and Mushroom Stuffing (page 48)

Pheasant Pilaf

75g/3oz dried apricots
75g/3oz prunes
1 pheasant, roasted and cooled
225g/8oz long-grain rice
salt and pepper
50g/2oz butter
75g/3oz blanched almonds
75g/3oz seedless raisins
2 eggs, beaten
30ml/2tbsp clear honey
30ml/2tbsp chopped parsley

Soak the apricots and prunes overnight. Stone the prunes if necessary. The pheasant can be roasted a day in advance, cooled then chilled. Timings are given for roasting on page 27. Remove the pheasant meat from the bones and dice it. Cook the rice in boiling salted water for 12–15 minutes, until tender. Drain well.

Heat the butter in a frying pan and brown the almonds lightly. Drain and add the soaked fruits and raisins. Add the pheasant meat and heat through for 5 minutes. Add the eggs with the cooked rice and all the remaining ingredients. Cook, stirring frequently, until the eggs are lightly set. Serve at once.

SERVES 4

MRS BEETON'S TIP

The pilaf, a rich, fruity rice dish, is an excellent recipe for using leftover pheasant. If you roast 2 birds and serve the breast meat only when freshly cooked, then the remains can be used in the pilaf.

Roast Marinated Grouse

A grouse can be cut in half lengthways through the breast-bone and spine, to make two helpings. Each half is served cut side down. If necessary, a third helping can be carved by removing the legs and thighs with a small portion of extra meat such as the 'oyster' on the back, before splitting the bird.

a brace of grouse
Red Wine Marinade (page 171) (optional)
50 g/2 oz butter
salt and pepper
2 rashers rindless streaky bacon
fat for basting
2 croûtes fried bread, each big enough to put under 1 bird
flour for dredging
watercress sprigs to garnish

Marinate the birds overnight or for 24 hours if home-shot or at all tough. Drain and reserve the marinade which can be added to the gravy and simmered briefly before serving.

Set the oven at 375°F/190°C/gas 5. Cream the butter with enough salt and pepper to give a good flavour, and put half into the body of each bird. Truss for roasting. Cover the breast of each bird with a bacon rasher. Place on a trivet or rack in a roasting tin, and roast for about 30 minutes, until tender. Baste with fat several times while cooking.

Halfway through the cooking time, put the croûtes in the tin, under the birds. Remove the bacon 7–8 minutes before the end of the cooking time and dredge the birds lightly with flour. Baste well and return to the oven to finish cooking and to brown. Serve the birds on the croûtes and garnish with watercress sprigs.

Serve thin gravy, Bread Sauce (page 161), and fried breadcrumbs separately.

SERVES 2

Roast Blackcock with Rosemary

The breast and thighs are the best meat on a blackcock. Carve the breast
into thin slices as for chicken or, if the bird is small, detach the
breast whole and slice it in half.

50g/2oz butter
salt and pepper
2 blackcock
10ml/2tsp finely chopped rosemary
4 rashers streaky bacon
2 croûtes fried bread, each big enough to put under 1 bird
watercress sprigs or *lemon wedges to garnish*

Set the oven at 375°F/190°C/gas 5. Cream the butter with salt and pepper to
taste. Put the seasoned butter in the birds, truss them, and sprinkle with the
rosemary. Cover the breasts with bacon. Roast on a rack for 45–50
minutes, basting frequently.

Halfway through the cooking time, put the croûtes in the tin, under the
birds. When the birds are almost cooked, remove the bacon and raise the
heat to brown the breasts. Serve garnished with watercress sprigs or lemon
wedges, on the croûtes of fried bread.

Serve thin gravy, Bread Sauce (page 161), and fried breadcrumbs
separately.

SERVES 6

MRS BEETON'S TIP

For a full-flavoured result cream 1 crushed clove of garlic
with the butter and seasoning.

Roast Pigeons

3 young woodpigeons
75g/3oz butter
lemon juice to taste • salt and pepper
3 small rashers rindless streaky bacon
3 croûtes fried bread, each big enough to put under 1 bird

Set the oven at 375°F/190°C/gas 5. Wipe the birds with a damp cloth. Mix the butter, lemon juice, and seasoning to taste. Insert 25g/1oz butter in each bird. Truss for roasting and cover each bird with a bacon rasher. Roast the pigeons for 20–30 minutes, or until tender. Baste while cooking, if necessary. Remove the bacon 10 minutes before the end of the cooking time to allow the birds to brown. When they are done, remove the trussing strings and replace the bacon. Serve each bird on a croûte of fried bread

SERVES 3

Juniper Spatchcocked Pigeons

3 young pigeons
45ml/3tbsp butter
salt and pepper
6 juniper berries, crushed

Split the birds down the back. Lay them out, flattening the breast with the skin side down, and skewer them flat. Melt the butter and brush the birds all over with the melted fat. Season to taste and sprinkle with the crushed juniper. Grill the pigeons for 20 minutes, turning them frequently.

Serve very hot and offer Fresh Tomato Sauce (page 168) or Mushroom Sauce (page 166) separately.

SERVES 6

Top: Roast Pigeons; Below: Pigeon Cutlets with Espagnole Sauce (overleaf)

Pigeon Cutlets with Espagnole Sauce

Illustrated on previous page

salt and pepper
3 pigeons
45ml/3tbsp butter or corn oil
stuffing made with 100g/4oz chicken livers
(see Braised Stuffed Duck, page 124)
2 eggs, beaten
breadcrumbs for coating
butter for greasing
300ml/½ pint Espagnole Sauce (page 162)

Season the meat well and fold each half bird into a neat cutlet shape. Heat the butter or oil in a frying pan. Fry the birds lightly on both sides to seal them and press between two plates until cold. Spread one side of each half pigeon with the stuffing. Coat the portions twice with egg and breadcrumbs. Leave to set in the refrigerator.

Set the oven at 350°F/180°C/ gas 4. Place the pigeons in a shallow greased tin, cover with buttered paper and cook for 20–30 minutes. If liked, pipe a border of Duchesse potato mixture round a dish, glaze and brown it. Place the cutlets in the centre, pour the Espagnole Sauce round them, then garnish with small piles of green vegetables.

SERVES 6

MRS BEETON'S TIP

To prepare pigeon cutlets, cut the feet off the pigeons. Split the birds in half lengthways and remove all the bones except the leg bones. Use a sharp pointed knife for this, sliding it between the breast meat and the bones. Cut off the wings and cut the remaining bones where they join to the legs.

Pigeon Cutlets with Spicy Sausagemeat

2 pigeons
40g/1 1/2 oz butter
salt and pepper
100g/4oz pork sausagement
1 small garlic clove, crushed
30ml/2tbsp chopped parsley
pinch of ground mace
2 eggs, beaten
breadcrumbs for coating
oil or fat for deep frying
300ml/1/2 pint Espagnole Sauce (page 162)

GARNISH

lime or lemon wedges
Macédoine of Vegetables (page 172)

Prepare, shape and fry the cutlets in the butter as for Pigeon Cutlets with Espagnole Sauce. Season the sausagemeat well, then mix the garlic, parsley and mace into it. Spread one side of each cutlet with the seasoned sausagemeat. Coat the cutlets with the beaten egg and breadcrumbs twice (the second coating prevents the sausagement from splitting away). Chill the cutlets well to seal the coating. Heat the oil or fat and fry the cutlets until well browned and cooked through.

Serve very hot with a Macédoine of Vegetables (page 172) and lime or lemon wedges to garnish.

SERVES 4

Devilled Partridge

If you like, take advantage of the wide variety of lettuce leaves that are now available to make a simple, yet interesting salad accompaniment for these partridges. For a complete contrast in texture, add slices of avocado to the salad.

2 partridges
30ml/2tbsp lemon juice
50g/2oz butter, melted
5ml/1tsp Dijon mustard
salt
cayenne pepper

GARNISH
grilled tomatoes
grilled mushrooms

Split the birds in half and wipe the insides thoroughly with a clean damp cloth. Mix the lemon juice, butter and mustard, then brush the mixture over the skin side of the birds. Season with salt and a little cayenne pepper. Grill the birds for 20–30 minutes, turning frequently. While the birds are cooking the tomatoes and mushrooms can be placed under the grill.

Serve the birds freshly cooked with the tomatoes and mushrooms. Sauté potatoes and a crisp fresh salad are excellent accompaniments.

SERVES 4

MRS BEETON'S TIP

A gentle combination of spicy ingredients is used to flavour these partridges. Dijon mustard has a mild flavour quite unlike that of hot, English mustard. You may like to increase the quantity of mustard to 10 ml/2 tsp. However, take care if you are unaccustomed to the taste of cayenne pepper, as it is very hot and, unless you favour hotly spiced dishes, it should be used in very small quantities.

Top: Roast Snipe with Port Wine Sauce (page 69); Below: Devilled Partridge

Roast Partridges Stuffed with Juniper

Illustrated on page 63

4 young partridges
juice of 1 lemon
a thin sheet of pork fat for barding
50g/2oz butter
45ml/3tbsp dry white wine
150ml/¼ pint Game Stock (page 40)
flour for dredging and for making gravy
4 large slices white bread from a tin loaf (optional)
butter for shallow frying
extra Game Stock for gravy

STUFFING
10 juniper berries
100g/4oz ham
1 small onion, chopped
grated rind of 1 lemon
50g/2oz butter
1 egg, beaten
pinch of dried marjoram
50g/2oz soft white breadcrumbs
salt and pepper

GARNISH
watercress sprigs
potato straws or fried breadcrumbs
lemon wedges (optional)

Make the stuffing first. Crush the juniper berries and shred the ham. Mix the crushed berries, ham, onions and lemon rind in a bowl. Melt the butter and add it to the bowl. Mix the beaten egg in with the marjoram and breadcrumbs. Mix in well with the ingredients in the bowl. Season well with salt and pepper. Use the mixture to stuff the birds.

Set the oven at 375°F/190°C/gas 5. Truss the birds for roasting, sprinkle with a little of the lemon juice and bard them with the pork fat. Put into a roasting tin, Melt the butter and brush it over the birds. Add the wine and

150 ml/¼ pint Game Stock to the tin and roast for 45 minutes, basting often with the pan juices. About 15 minutes before the end of the cooking time, remove the pork barding fat. Dredge the birds lightly with a little flour, then return them to the oven to finish cooking and to brown.

If you like, the partridges can be served, traditional style, on slices of fried bread. Prepare these fried bread croûtes at this stage, while the birds are browning. Fry the bread slices in butter until golden and lightly crisped, cut off the crusts and keep aside.

When the birds are cooked, place each on a croûte of fried bread (if used), and arrange them on a serving dish with their drumsticks in the centre. Keep warm under buttered paper while making the gravy. Skim the fat off the pan juices, sprinkle in a little flour, and place over a moderate heat. Stir for 2 minutes, scraping in any sediment. Stir in enough of the remaining Game Stock to make a thin, well-flavoured gravy.

Garnish the birds with a bunch of watercress sprigs in the centre of the dish. Place small piles of potato straws or fried breadcrumbs between them, and lemon wedges on top, if you like.

Serve the gravy separately in a warmed sauceboat. As well as, or instead of the gravy you may like to serve Bread Sauce (page 161) or Cumberland Sauce (page 165). Redcurrant jelly is another traditional accompaniment that should be offered with the birds.

SERVES 4

MRS BEETON'S TIP

A partridge may be cut in half lengthways through the breast-bone and spine. Although a partridge is seldom large enough to serve more than two people, a third portion can be carved, if necessary, in the same way as grouse, by serving the legs with a small portion of meat, such as the 'oyster' from the back of the bird.

Normandy Partridges

Serve simple, but interesting, vegetables to accompany this old-fashioned French dish. Tiny scrubbed potatoes, baked in their jackets, lightly steamed French beans and carrots cut into thin, julienne strips are all ideal.

100g/4oz unsalted butter
2 young partridges
salt and pepper
2 rashers rindless streaky bacon
700g/1½ lb dessert apples
100ml/4floz double cream
30ml/2tbsp Calvados or brandy
chopped parsley to garnish

Heat half the butter in a flameproof casserole, add the partridges and brown them on all sides. Sprinkle with salt and pepper. Place a bacon rasher on each bird's breast. Set the oven at 350°F/180°C/gas 4. Peel, core and cut the apples into wedges. Melt the remaining butter in a pan, add the apples and cover the pan. Cook gently for 5 minutes, then add to the casserole.

Cook in the oven for 20–30 minutes. Transfer the partridges and apples to a hot serving dish.

Mix the cream and the Calvados or brandy, then season to taste. Heat the mixture over a low heat, stirring well, and taking care that the mixture does not boil. Pour this sauce over the apples, and sprinkle with chopped parsley before serving.

SERVES 2

MRS BEETON'S TIP

Calvados is a brandy which is prepared by distilling cider. It is made in the Auge region of France and is an essential ingredient in a variety of traditional dishes from Normandy.

Top: Roast Partridges Stuffed with Juniper (page 60); Below: Normandy Partridges

Roast Quail in a Vine-leaf Coat

Illustrated on page 66

8 oven-ready quail
8 fresh or canned vine leaves
8 rashers rindless streaky bacon
4 large slices bread from a tin loaf
butter for spreading
small bunches of black and green grapes to garnish

Set the oven at 400°F/200°C/gas 6. Wrap each quail in a vine leaf. Wrap one rasher of bacon round each quail. Secure with thread or wooden cocktail sticks. Place on a rack in a roasting tin and roast for 10–12 minutes.

   Meanwhile, cut the crusts off the bread, cut each slice in half and toast lightly on both sides. Spread the toast with drippings from the quail and a little butter. Serve each quail on toast and garnish with grapes.

SERVES 4

Brandied Quail with Grapes

8 oven-ready quail
25g/1oz flour • 30ml/2tbsp brandy
225g/8oz seedless green grapes

STUFFING
liver from quails (optional)
60ml/4tbsp diced cooked bacon
90ml/6tbsp soft white breadcrumbs
squeeze of lemon juice
salt and pepper

First make the stuffing. Fry the quails' livers, if available. Chop up well and add the bacon and breadcrumbs, mixing well together. Add the lemon juice and season to taste.

Set the oven at 400°F/200°C/gas 6. Place the stuffing in the quail and roast for 14–18 minutes. When the quail are cooked, remove from the roasting tin or rack. Make a thick gravy using the pan juices and the flour. Add the brandy, then the grapes to the gravy. Season to taste before serving. Arrange the quail on a serving platter, with the grape sauce poured around them.

SERVES 4

Fillets of Duck Bigarade

Illustrated overleaf

1 duck
350g/12oz Duchesse Potatoes (page 170)
1 small orange
300ml/½ pint Bigarade Sauce (page 169)

Set the oven at 400°F/200°C/gas 6. Truss the duck, and roast it for 1–1½ hours, or until tender, basting occasionally.

Pipe the potato mixture in a border on the serving dish, brown it in the oven and keep hot. Coursely grate the rind of the orange, add to the Bigarade sauce and keep hot. Slice the orange and set aside.

Remove the breast from the duck. Cut it into neat strips while still hot and arrange them overlapping each other within the potato border. Pour the sauce over the duck and garnish with the orange slices.

SERVES 2

*Top: Fillets of Duck Bigarade (previous page); Below: Roast Quail
in a Vine-leaf Coat (page 64)*

Spicy Roast Duck

1 duck
1 small onion
4 cloves
1 cinnamon stick
butter for basting
30ml/2tbsp flour for dredging
freshly grated nutmeg
salt and pepper
1 large slice of white bread to fit under the bird
watercress sprigs to garnish

Set the oven at 375°F/190°C/gas 5. Cut off the toes of the bird, and scald and scrape the feet. Stud the onion with the cloves, then place it in the body cavity of the bird with the cinnamon stick. Truss the bird with the feet twisted underneath the body. Warm the butter until melted and brush the bird all over with melted butter. Mix the flour, some grated nutmeg and seasoning. Dredge the duck lightly with the seasoned flour. Place on a trivet in a roasting tin, baste with any remaining butter and roast for 20–30 minutes. Baste often during cooking.

As soon as the bird is in the oven, cut the crusts off the bread and toast it lightly on both sides. Place it while still warm in the roasting tin, under the bird.

Remove the bird and the bread croûte from the oven as soon as it is tender. Serve it slightly underdone, or the flavour will be lost. Place on a heated serving dish and garnish with watercress sprigs just before serving.

SERVES 3

MRS BEETON'S TIP

Carve the breast like that of farmed duck. Remove the wings without any extra meat above the joint, and discard them. Remove the legs in the same way as a chicken's, and cut in half at the joint. Serve only the thighs.

Teal with Orange Salad

Illustrated on page 71

2 teal
1 orange
50g/2oz unsalted butter
2 slices white bread
cayenne pepper
lemon juice
flour for dredging
thyme sprigs to garnish

ORANGE SALAD
2 small sweet oranges
5ml/1tsp caster sugar
15ml/1tbsp french dressing
brandy (optional)

Set the oven at 425°F/220°C/gas 7. Prepare the birds as for Spicy Roast Duck. Before trussing them, quarter the orange and put some inside each bird. Melt the butter and brush the birds with it. Place them on a trivet in a roasting tin, baste them and pour any remaining butter into the tin. Roast the teal for 20 minutes, basting often.

As soon as the birds are in the oven, cut the crusts off the bread, toast lightly on both sides and place the slices under the birds in the tin. At the same time, sprinkle the birds lightly with cayenne pepper and lemon juice.

About 5 minutes before the end of the cooking time, sprinkle the birds with flour. Baste well and return them to the oven until the flour froths and the breasts are well coloured.

Make the salad. Let the oranges stand in boiling water for 2 minutes, turning them over once. Peel them and remove all the white pith. Cut into segments, discarding the pips and membranes. Sprinkle the segments with sugar, french dressing and a very little brandy, if liked.

Serve the birds on the croûtes of bread, and garnish with orange salad and thyme sprigs. Serve Bigarade Sauce (page 169) separately.

SERVES 2

Roast Snipe with Port Wine Sauce

3 snipe
40g/1½ oz butter
3 thin rashers bacon
3 slices toast
butter for basting
flour for dredging
300ml/½ pint Foundation Brown Sauce (page 160)
juice of 1 lemon
about 100ml/4fl oz port

GARNISH
endive leaves
lemon wedges or *slices*

Set the oven at 375°F/190°C/gas 5. Truss the birds as described on page 26. Do not draw them. Melt the butter and brush the birds with it. Tie a bacon rasher over each bird's breast. Place the slices of toast in a roasting tin to catch the juices (the trail) as they drop from the birds. Place a roasting rack or trivet over them and put the birds on it. Roast for 15–20 minutes – the snipe should be served slightly underdone but this is a matter for personal taste. Baste the birds frequently with butter.

Shortly before serving, remove the bacon. Dredge the birds lightly with flour and baste well to brown the breasts lightly. Return to the oven to finish cooking.

Meanwhile, heat the Foundation Brown Sauce; add the lemon juice and the port. Serve the birds on the toast, and garnish with endive and lemon wedges or slices. Serve the sauce separately.

SERVES 3

MRS BEETON'S TIP

Melted clarified butter, flavoured with lemon juice, can be served instead of brown sauce. Snipe can be divided into two portions by cutting lengthways through the breast-bone and spine, after removing the head.

Stuffed Roast Hare

1 hare, with liver
Basic Forcemeat (page 172)
4 rashers streaky bacon
milk for basting
butter for basting (optional)
50g/2oz butter
1 small shallot, chopped
5ml/1tsp chopped parsley
pinch of dried thyme
40g/1½ oz flour
450ml/¾ pint All-purpose Stock (page 40)
salt and pepper
about 100ml/4fl oz port (optional)
flour for dredging
1 stuffed olive, halved, to garnish

Set the oven at 400°F/200°C/gas 6. Stuff the hare with the forcemeat and sew up securely. Truss the hare. Place on a rack in a roasting tin. Cover it with the streaky bacon and roast for 1½–2 hours, or until tender. Baste frequently with milk and a little butter, if liked.

Meanwhile, prepare the liver. Put it into cold water, bring to the boil and boil for 5 minutes. Chop it very finely. Melt the butter, add the liver, shallot, parsley and thyme. Fry for 10 minutes. Remove the liver mixture from the butter. Stir in the flour and brown the roux well. Stir in the stock gradually. Bring to boiling point and add the liver mixture. Season to taste, then simmer for 10 minutes. Add the wine, if used.

Remove the bacon from the hare and dredge with flour. Baste and return to the oven to continue cooking for 10–15 minutes, to allow the hare to brown. Remove the trussing strings and skewers. Take the covering off the head and ears. Place half a stuffed olive in each eye socket. Serve the hare on a heated dish.

Serve the liver sauce and forcement stuffing separately.

SERVES 5 TO 6

Teal with Orange Salad (page 68)

Baked Hare with Mushroom Stuffing

1 shallot
225g/8oz pickled or salt pork
225g/8oz pie veal
a little All-purpose Stock (page 40)
salt and pepper
75ml/3fl oz sherry (optional)
225g/8oz flat well-flavoured mushrooms, chopped
1 young hare
lard for basting

Set the oven at 400°F/200°C/gas 6. Mince the shallot with the pork and veal. Moisten with a little stock, season to taste and add the sherry, if used. Add the mushrooms to the stuffing. Press the stuffing lightly into the body of the hare, sew up the opening, and truss into shape.

Heat the lard in a roasting tin in the oven. Baste the hare well with the hot fat, cover with 2–3 sheets of greased greaseproof paper and bake for 1–1¼ hours. Baste frequently while cooking. About 20 minutes before serving, remove the paper and allow the hare to brown. When the meat is cooked, remove any skewers and string.

S E R V E S 5 T O 6

Roast Leveret

2 leverets
butter for basting
flour for dredging
300ml/½ pint All-purpose Stock (page 40)

Set the oven at 375°F/190°C/gas 5. Truss the leverets as for a hare but do not stuff them. Roast them for 50–60 minutes, basting them often with butter. Dredge with flour 10–15 minutes before serving, baste again and leave to brown.

When ready, remove the trussing strings. Keep hot, while making gravy with the stock and pan drippings. Serve the leverets with the gravy.

Serve redcurrant jelly separately. A purée of chestnuts or braised red cabbage makes a good accompaniment.

SERVES 5 TO 6

Barbecue of Rabbit

1 large rabbit
salt and pepper
butter or olive oil
60ml/4tbsp tomato ketchup
15ml/1tbsp lemon juice
50ml/2fl oz red wine
50ml/2fl oz tomato juice
5ml/1tsp prepared French mustard
30ml/2tbsp Demerara sugar
dash of Tabasco sauce
lemon slices to garnish

Leave the rabbit in salted water for 1 hour, then dry it thoroughly. Make slits with a knife point in the flesh of the back and legs, then rub salt and pepper into them. Melt the butter, if used. Brush the rabbit all over with butter or oil.

Heat the ketchup with the remaining ingredients. Check the seasoning, then brush some of the sauce over the rabbit. Grill the rabbit for 20–25 minutes, basting it with the sauce and turning it often. When tender and brown, divide it into neat joints and place them on a hot dish. Pour the cooking juices and sauce over them. Garnish with the lemon.

SERVES 3 TO 4

Roast Rabbit with Potato Dice

6 potatoes
1 rabbit
Basic Forcemeat (page 172)
4 rashers streaky bacon
fat for basting
4 – 8 bacon rolls
Fresh Tomato Sauce (page 168) to serve
watercress sprigs to garnish

Cut the potatoes into 1.25- cm/½- inch cubes and blanch them in boiling salted water for 2 minutes. Drain and set aside.

Set the oven at 400°F/200°C/gas 6. Stuff the rabbit with the forcemeat, skewer up the cavity opening and truss. Cover the back with the bacon rashers. Heat the fat in the oven, in the roasting tin to be used for the rabbit. Brush the rabbit with the hot fat and put it into the tin. Roast the rabbit for 1–1½ hours, depending on its size. Baste it often while cooking.

About 30 minutes before the end of the cooking time, put the potatoes into the roasting tin with the meat. Baste them well and cook with the meat until tender and browned, turning them over often while cooking. About 10 minutes before the rabbit is ready, remove the bacon rashers from the back, to let the meat brown. At the same time put the bacon rolls in a small baking tin and place in the oven on the rack below the rabbit to bake in their own fat. Meanwhile, prepare the Fresh Tomato Sauce.

When the rabbit is cooked, remove the skewers or string from trussing. Place it on a heated dish and pour a little of the sauce round it. Alternatively portion the rabbit before arranging it on the dish. Garnish with small piles of the potato and with the bacon rolls and watercress sprigs. Serve the remaining sauce separately.

SERVES 4

Roast Rabbit with Potato Dice

Sandringham Rabbit

1 rabbit
salt and pepper
2 large tomatoes
1 small shallot, chopped
5ml/1tsp grated lemon rind
50g/2oz soft white breadcrumbs
5ml/1tsp chopped parsley
2.5ml/½ tsp dried thyme
50g/2oz shredded suet
1 egg, beaten
1 rasher bacon
30ml/2tbsp cooking oil for basting
bacon rolls to garnish

Set the oven at 400°F/200°C/gas 6. Season the rabbit well. Peel the tomatoes and chop them finely. Mix the tomatoes with the shallot, lemon rind, breadcrumbs, parsley, thyme and suet. Bind the mixture with the egg. Stuff the rabbit with the mixture and truss it using the simpler method. Lay the bacon rasher on top of the rabbit. Brush with some of the oil.

Roast the rabbit for 50–60 minutes, basting with the oil from time to time. Remove the bacon about 10 minutes before serving to let the meat brown. At the same time, put the bacon rolls in the oven in a small baking tin to cook until crisp. When the meat is cooked, remove the trussing strings or skewers. Serve the rabbit garnished with the bacon rolls.

Serve Fresh Tomato Sauce (page 168) or Foundation Brown Sauce (page 160) separately.

SERVES 3 TO 4

Roast Haunch of Venison

a haunch of venison
clarified butter or *dripping*
flour for dredging

Set the oven at 350°F/180°C/gas 4. Trim the bone end off the venison and cut off all the fat. Melt the clarified butter or dripping and brush the joint well all over, then wrap in well-greased aluminium foil or a sheet of greaseproof paper. If using paper, make a stiff paste of flour and water and cover the joint with it, then cover with another well-greased sheet of paper and tie securely with string.

Roast the joint on a rack for 15 minutes per 450g/1lb for large joints, 20 minutes per 450g/1lb for smaller joints weighing 1.4kg/3lb or less. About 20–30 minutes before the cooking time is completed, remove the foil or paste and papers, dredge lightly with flour and baste well with hot butter. Continue cooking until the joint is tender and a good brown colour.

Have the traditional or other accompaniments ready before removing the venison from the oven. Transfer to a heated carving dish and serve at once.

SERVES 6 TO 8

MRS BEETON'S TIP

Fat is clarified in order to remove impurities and water from it. Clarified butter has good keeping qualities and it can be stored in a covered container in the refrigerator for at least a month. It is an ingredient which is widely used in Indian cooking, in which recipes it is usually referred to as ghee. Melt butter over a low heat and simmer it gently for about 15 minutes, taking care not to overheat it. Strain the butter through double-thick muslin, leaving the sediment in the bottom of the pan. Absorbent kitchen paper can be used instead of muslin.

Roast Venison with Baked Apples

4 small sharp cooking apples, peeled and cored
juice of 1 lemon
30ml/2tbsp gooseberry, rowanberry or redcurrant jelly
15ml/1tbsp butter
10ml/2tsp soft brown sugar
1kg/2lb young venison
about 45ml/3tbsp oil

S A U C E
150ml/¼ pint All-purpose Stock (page 40)
30ml/2tbsp gooseberry, rowanberry or redcurrant jelly
small pinch of ground cloves
salt and pepper
10ml/2tsp cornflour
15ml/1tbsp cold water
30ml/2tbsp sherry

Simmer the apples gently in a little water with the lemon juice for 10–15 minutes. Drain and arrange in an ovenproof dish. Fill the core holes with the gooseberry, rowanberry or redcurrant jelly. Dot each apple with a small piece of butter, and sprinkle with the brown sugar.

Set the oven at 375°F/190°C/gas 5. Brush the venison with 30ml/2tbsp of the oil and roast with the apples for 40 minutes, basting with extra oil from time to time.

Meanwhile, make the sauce. Put the stock, jelly, ground cloves, salt and pepper in a small pan. Heat gently to dissolve the jelly. Blend the cornflour with the water, add to the stock and bring to the boil, stirring all the time. Cook for 2 minutes to thicken and clear the sauce.

Slice the meat and arrange it on a warm dish with the apples; keep both hot. Place the pan in which the meat was cooked over the heat, add the sauce and the sherry and scrape together with the pan drippings. Strain over the meat.

S E R V E S   4   T O   6

Partridges with Cabbage (page 91)

Fried Venison Cutlets

If you favour the flavour of olive oil, then the coated cutlets can be cooked in the oil in which they were marinated, instead of using the butter.

8 cutlets of venison from leg or loin
75ml/5tbsp olive oil
60ml/4tbsp flour
salt and pepper
1 egg, beaten
75g/3oz dried breadcrumbs
75g/3oz butter
8 large mushrooms
100g/4oz redcurrant jelly
10ml/2tsp red wine vinegar
5ml/1tsp Demerara sugar

Marinate the cutlets in the oil for about 1 hour. Drain well. Season the flour with salt and pepper and use to coat each cutlet. Coat each cutlet first in the beaten egg and then in the crumbs, pressing them on well. Heat 40g/1½ oz of the butter and fry the cutlets for about 10–12 minutes, adding more butter if necessary and turning once or twice. Drain and keep hot.

Heat the remaining butter and fry the mushrooms; place a mushroom on each cutlet. Mix the jelly, vinegar and sugar with the pan juices. Heat the jelly to melt it and reduce it a little. Serve with the cutlets.

SERVES 8

MRS BEETON'S TIP

For the very best results when coating foods in egg and breadcrumbs, it is essential to have fine, dried white crumbs. Make the crumbs from fresh bread, then dry them in a cool oven until they are crisp. Process them in a food processor or blender, or rub them against the inside of a metal sieve, to make sure they are fine.

Cutlets of Minced Venison

Although these cutlets of minced venison are intended as a main dish, they also make an unusual starter if the mixture is shaped into eight small portions before cooking.

450g/1lb venison
3 small onions, quartered
5ml/1tsp chopped parsley
pinch of freshly grated nutmeg
1 egg, beaten
salt and pepper
flour for coating
25g/1oz butter
15ml/1tbsp oil

GARNISH
fried tomato halves
watercress sprigs

Cut the meat into small pieces. Mince together the meat and onions coarsely. Stir in the parsley, nutmeg, egg and seasoning. Form into four flat cakes, the size and shape of cutlets, then coat lightly with flour. Chill well before cooking.

Heat the butter and oil in a frying pan, put in the cutlets and fry gently for 10 minutes. Turn over and fry for another 7–10 minutes. Drain and serve at once, garnished with the tomatoes and watercress sprigs.

SERVES 4

Polish Fried Venison

An accompaniment of simply cooked white cabbage will complement these sauced venison steaks. Toss finely shredded white cabbage with a chopped onion in a little oil until just tender, then season to taste before serving.

6 juniper berries
60ml/4tbsp wine vinegar
30ml/2tbsp Game Stock (page 40)
250ml/8fl oz Velouté Sauce (page 165)
salt and pepper
40g/1½ oz butter
6 thick slices leg of venison

Crush the juniper berries and simmer them in the vinegar until the liquid is reduced by half. Add the stock and the sauce and cook gently for 15 minutes. Strain the sauce and season it. Stir in half the butter and keep hot under damp paper.

Flatten the venison slices with a meat mallet, heat the rest of the butter and fry them for 10–15 minutes, turning once. Arrange the steaks on a hot dish and pour some of the sauce over them. Serve the rest separately in a heated sauceboat.

SERVES 6

MRS BEETON'S TIP

To flatten meat, place it between two sheets of greaseproof paper and bat it out until it is as thin as required. A meat mallet can be used, alternatively a rolling pin will work just as well.

CASSEROLES
AND STEWS

Stewed Pheasant with Chestnut Stuffing

1 pheasant
600ml/1pint Game Stock (page 40)
1 onion
1 carrot
½ small turnip
1 bouquet garni

STUFFING
450g/1lb chestnuts or 225g/8oz shelled or canned chestnuts
50 – 150ml/2 – 5fl oz stock
25g/1oz butter
salt and pepper
pinch of ground cinnamon
1.25ml/¼ tsp sugar

First make the stuffing. Make a slit in the rounded side of the chestnuts in their shells and bake or boil them for 20 minutes. Remove the shells and skins while hot. Put the chestnuts in a saucepan with just enough stock to cover them. Heat to boiling point, reduce the heat, cover, and stew until the chestnuts are tender. Drain and reserve the stock. Rub the chestnuts through a fine wire sieve into a bowl. Add the butter, seasoning, cinnamon and sugar. Stir in enough stock to make a soft stuffing.

Fill the cavity of the bird with the chestnut stuffing. Truss the bird for roasting. Bring the stock to the boil. Wrap the bird securely in well-greased aluminium foil, then put the bird into the boiling stock. Bring back to boiling point, add the vegetables and bouquet garni, reduce the heat and simmer gently for about 1 hour. Remove the trussing strings and serve the bird on a hot dish immediately.

SERVES 4

Pheasant with Oysters

1 pheasant
600ml/1pint chicken stock
1 onion, sliced
1 carrot, sliced
½ small turnip, diced
1 bouquet garni
450ml/¾ pint Oyster Sauce (page 168)

O Y S T E R   S T U F F I N G
6 fresh or canned oysters
100g/4oz soft white breadcrumbs
50g/2oz shredded suet or butter
5ml/1tsp chopped fresh mixed herbs
pinch of freshly grated nutmeg
salt and pepper
1 egg, beaten

First make the stuffing. If using fresh oysters, simmer them very gently in their own liquor for 10 minutes. Canned oysters need no cooking. Drain and reserve a little liquor. Cut the oysters into small pieces. Mix the breadcrumbs with the suet or butter, then add the oysters, herbs, nutmeg and seasoning to taste. Bind with the egg and the reserved oyster liquor, if necessary.

Fill the cavity of the bird with the oyster stuffing. Truss the bird for roasting. Bring the stock to boiling point. Wrap the bird securely in well-greased foil, then put the bird into the boiling stock. Bring back to boiling point, add the sliced vegetables and bouquet garni to the pan, reduce the heat and simmer gently for about 1 hour. Remove the trussing strings and serve the bird on a hot dish with a little oyster sauce poured round. Serve the rest of the sauce in a sauce-boat.

S E R V E S   4   T O   5

Pheasant Veronique

If you are following a low-fat diet, or simply taking care to avoid over indulging in rich foods, then this dish can easily be adapted to suit the menu. Omit the butter and substitute fromage frais for the double cream. Do not reheat the sauce once the fromage frais is stirred in.

2 pheasants
salt and pepper
75g/3oz butter
600ml/1pint chicken stock
7.5–10 ml/1½–2tsp arrowroot
25g/8oz seedless white grapes, peeled
60ml/4tbsp double cream
5ml/1tsp lemon juice

Set the oven at 350°F/180°C/gas 4. Wipe the pheasants, season and rub well all over with butter. Put a knob of butter inside each bird. Place the pheasants, breast side down, in a deep pot roaster or flameproof casserole. Cover with stock and buttered paper. Cook for 1 – 1¼ hours, until tender, turning the birds breast side up after 25 minutes.

When cooked, remove the pheasants from the stock and cut into convenient portions for serving; keep hot. Boil the liquid in the casserole to reduce it a little. Strain into a saucepan. Blend the arrowroot with a little water, then stir it into the hot stock. Bring to the boil and stir until the sauce thickens and clears. Add the grapes, cream and lemon juice, then heat through without boiling. Check the seasoning. Arrange the pheasants on a serving dish with the sauce spooned over them.

SERVES 4 TO 6

MRS BEETON'S TIP

When seedless grapes are not available, halve ordinary fruit and remove all the seeds. Unfortunately, this is a tedious task which is essential to the success of the dish. Use a small, pointed knife to peel the grapes.

Top: Pheasant Veronique; Below: Pigeons in Red Wine (overleaf)

Pigeons in Red Wine

Illustrated on previous page

75 g/3 oz butter
3 woodpigeons
300 ml/½ pint Foundation Brown Sauce (page 160)
about 300 ml/½ pint red wine
salt and pepper
1 large onion or 3 shallots, sliced

Heat two-thirds of the butter and fry the pigeons, turning as required, until browned on all sides. Heat the brown sauce and wine to simmering point in a saucepan. Put the pigeons into the sauce and simmer with the pan half-covered for about 45 minutes, or until the birds are tender. Taste and season just before serving.

Melt the remaining butter and fry the onion or shallots. Drain well and keep hot. Split the cooked pigeons in half and serve half to each person with the onions and the sauce poured over them.

SERVES 6

Pigeon Casserole

4 rashers rindless streaky bacon
4 young pigeons
50g/2oz butter or margarine
225g/8oz button onions
40g/1½ oz plain flour
300ml/½ pint beef stock
15ml/1tbsp concentrated tomato purée
225g/8oz button mushrooms
salt and pepper
chopped parsley to garnish

Cut the bacon into strips. Wipe and dry the pigeons. Heat the butter or margarine in a frying pan and brown the pigeons all over.

Set the oven at 375°F/180°C/gas 4. Put the pigeons in a 2–litre/3½–pint casserole. Put the onions and bacon in the frying pan and brown lightly. Stir in the flour and gradually add the stock, then bring to the boil. Stir in the tomato purée, blend in thoroughly, then add the mushrooms and season well. Pour the mixture over the pigeons, cover and cook for 1–1½ hours, until the pigeons are tender. Lift them out and arrange on a heated serving dish. Spoon the sauce over them, and sprinkle with parsley.

S E R V E S   6   T O   8

Compôte of Pigeons

3 woodpigeons or *large pigeons*
100g/4oz ham or *bacon*
40g/1½ oz butter
3 shallots or *1 large onion, sliced*
600ml/1 pint Game Stock (page 40)
or *All-purpose Stock (page 40)*
1 bouquet garni
1 carrot, sliced • *½ turnip, diced*
25g/1oz flour • *salt and pepper*

Truss the pigeons for roasting. Cut the ham or bacon into small pieces. Heat the butter in a large pan and fry the pigeons, ham or bacon and onions until well browned. Add the stock and bring to boiling point. Add the bouquet garni, carrot and turnip. Cover, reduce the heat and simmer steadily for 1–1½ hours, or until the pigeons are tender. Blend the flour with a little stock and add to the pan. Bring to the boil, stirring continuously, then simmer for 10 minutes. Season and serve.

S E R V E S   6

Jugged Pigeons

3 woodpigeons
75g/3oz butter
1 small onion, chopped
600ml/1pint Game Stock (page 40)
salt and pepper
25g/1oz flour
about 100ml/4fl oz port or claret (optional)

GARNISH
fried Forcemeat Balls (page 172)
croûtons of fried bread
parsley sprigs

Set the oven at 320°F/160°C/gas 3. Truss the pigeons for roasting. Heat two-thirds of the butter and fry them in it until well browned. Remove the birds to a casserole, preferably earthenware. Brown the onion in the same butter as the pigeons. Add the onion to the pigeons, together with the stock and seasoning to taste. Cover and cook in the oven for 1¾ hours.

Knead together the flour and remaining butter to make a beurre manié paste and drop small pieces into the stock, stirring all the time. Continue cooking for a further 15 minutes. Add the wine, if used, and cook for another 15 minutes. Serve the pigeons with the sauce poured over them and garnish with forcemeat balls, croûtons and parsley.

SERVES 6

Partridges with Cabbage

1 cabbage, sliced
100g/4oz rashers rindless bacon
2 partridges
50g/2oz butter
2 cloves

225g/8oz frankfurter sausages
2 juniper berries
2 carrots, sliced
salt and pepper
pinch of freshly grated nutmeg
450ml/¾ pint Game Stock (page 40)
25g/1oz flour (optional)
25g/1oz butter (optional)

Parboil the cabbage in boiling salted water for 5 minutes. Drain well. Cut the bacon into small pieces. Prepare the birds for casseroling by tying or skewering the limbs to the body in a neat shape.

Set the oven at 275°F/140°C/gas 1. Melt the butter in a pan and brown the birds all over. Stick a clove in each onion. Put an onion in the body of each bird. Cook the bacon lightly in the pan. Cut the frankfurters into 2.5- cm/1- inch pieces. Crush the juniper berries.

Place a layer of cabbage in the base of a deep casserole and arrange the partridges on top with the bacon, sliced carrots, frankfurters and crushed Juniper. Season with salt, pepper and nutmeg. Cover with the remaining cabbage and pour in enough stock to come half-way up the casserole. Cover with buttered paper and a lid. Cook for 3–4 hours.

Arrange the birds on a bed of cabbage on a heated serving dish with the other ingredients from the casserole. Skim and strain the liquid from the casserole into a clean pan. Reduce it by boiling to the desired strength or, if preferred, make a beurre manié from the flour and butter and use to thicken the liquid.

SERVES 3 TO 4

Casserole of Duck with Peas

1 duck
salt and pepper
25g/1oz flour
4 shallots, finely chopped
100g/4oz mushrooms, finely chopped
about 450ml/³⁄4 pint All-purpose Stock (page 40)
225g/8oz fresh green peas
5ml/1tsp chopped mint

Set the oven at 400°F/200°C/gas 6. Joint and skin the duck. Season the flour and dip the joints in it. Put the shallots and mushrooms with the duck in a casserole. Just cover with stock, put on a tight-fitting lid and cook for 45 minutes. Add the peas and mint and continue cooking for about 30 minutes, until the duck is tender. Check the seasoning. Serve from the casserole.

SERVES 4

MRS BEETON'S TIP

In the preparation of this dish, the first step is to cut the uncooked duck into suitable serving portions. Place the duck breast down on a clean surface. Using a meat cleaver or heavy cook's knife, cut the bird in half down the back. Then cut through the breastbone underneath to separate the two halves. A pair of poultry shears or stout kitchen scissors are ideal for snipping through small bones. Cut each half into two portions, separating the legs and the wings, and cutting the majority of the breast meat with the wings. The skin is removed by pulling it away from the portions, easing the point of a knife in where it does not come away easily.

Duckling in Red Wine

1 duckling
salt and pepper
2 onions, finely chopped
1 bay leaf
250ml/8fl oz red wine
100g/4oz bacon
10ml/2tsp cooking oil
450ml/¾ pint stock
1 medium carrot, sliced
2 celery sticks, sliced
grated rind of 1 orange or lemon
100g/4oz button mushrooms

Cut the duckling into quarters and season well. Put the onions into a bowl with the duck quarters, bay leaf and red wine. Cover and leave to marinate for 2 hours. Remove the duck portions from the wine and dry on absorbent kitchen paper; strain and reserve the liquid.

Set the oven at 350°F/180°C/gas 4. Chop the bacon. Heat the oil in a pan and cook the bacon gently for 3–4 minutes. Add the duckling and brown it all over. Drain well and put in a casserole. Heat the stock and pour it into the casserole. Cook for 15 minutes.

Add the carrot and celery to the casserole with the grated rind, mushrooms and the reserved marinade. Cover and cook for 1½–2 hours, until tender. Skim off any surplus fat before serving.

SERVES 4

Olive Duck Casserole

Tart stuffed green olives complement the richness of duck
in this colourful casserole.

450ml/¾ pint water
giblets of 1 duck
6 small carrots
2 onions, chopped
1 bouquet garni
salt and pepper
1 duck
30ml/2tbsp goose, duck or chicken fat
2 slices stale white bread
24 stuffed green olives

Put the water in a saucepan with the duck giblets but reserve the liver (this can be used for another dish). Chop half the carrots and thinly slice the remaining ones. Add the chopped carrots and onions to the pan with the bouquet garni and seasoning to taste. Simmer, uncovered, for about 40 minutes to obtain about 350ml/12fl oz well-flavoured stock.

Meanwhile, season the inside of the duck. Heat the fat in a heavy, flameproof casserole, put in the duck and brown it on all sides. Reduce the heat, cover the casserole and cook slowly for 15 minutes. Remove the duck, joint it and return the joints to the casserole. Grate or crumble the bread, sprinkle it over the duck, then strain the stock over the dish. Plunge the olives into boiling water for 1 minute, then add them to the casserole. Add the sliced carrots also. Cover the casserole, place over a low heat and simmer for 45 minutes. Serve with plain boiled rice or saffron rice.

SERVES 4 TO 5

Top: Pigeon or Rabbit Pudding (page 146); Below: Grouse Pie (page 136)

Jugged Hare

Jugged hare is thickened with the blood which is saved when the animal is paunched. If you intend buying the hare, then ask the butcher to save the blood when you order the game.

1 hare
liver of the hare (optional)
blood of the hare (if obtainable)
5ml/1tsp vinegar (if required)
30ml/2tbsp flour
salt and pepper
100g/4oz butter or margarine
3 whole cloves
1 onion
1 bouquet garni
good pinch of ground mace
good pinch of freshly grated nutmeg
beef stock to moisten
150ml/¼ pint port or claret
50g/2oz redcurrant jelly
15ml/1tbsp butter (optional)
15ml/1tbsp flour (optional)
lemon juice (optional)

GARNISH

heart-shaped or triangular snippets of toasted bread
Forcemeat Balls (page 172)

Joint the hare. Reserve the liver and the blood. Mix the blood with the vinegar to prevent it coagulating. Set the oven at 350°F/180°C/gas 4. Season the flour with salt and pepper, then dust the hare joints with it. Heat the butter or margarine in a frying pan and brown the hare joints all over. Put to one side.

Press the cloves into the onion. Put the hare joints into a deep ovenproof pot or cooking jar, preferably earthenware. Add the onion, bouquet garni, spices and just enough stock to cover about a quarter of the joints. Cover the dish very securely with foil and stand it in a pan of very hot water. Cook for about 3 hours, depending on the age and toughness of the hare.

Meanwhile, prepare the liver. When the hare is cooked, remove the meat to a serving dish and keep hot. Pour off the juices into a smaller pan. Mash the hare's liver into the hot liquid, if using it. Add the port or claret and redcurrant jelly. If using the hare's blood to thicken the sauce, add it to the liquids in the pan and reheat, stirring all the time; do not allow it to boil. If not using the blood, mix the butter and flour to make a beurre manié. Heat the liquids in the pan to simmering point, remove from the heat and stir in the beurre manié in small spoonfuls. Return the pan to the heat and stir gently until the beurre manié is dissolved and the mixture boils and thickens. Sharpen with a few drops of lemon juice, if liked.

Pour the thickened sauce over the hare joints and serve garnished with the sippets and Forcemeat Balls.

SERVES 6

Top: Haricot of Hare (page 101); Below: Civet of Hare with Gammon

Civet of Hare with Gammon

forequarters, neck and breast of 1 hare
225g/8oz gammon
50g/2oz butter • 30ml/2tbsp flour
1 garlic clove • 1 bouquet garni
2.5ml/½ tsp sugar
salt and freshly ground black pepper
10 pickling onions
225g/8oz mushrooms
liver and blood of the hare

<u>MARINADE</u>
1 onion, thickly sliced
1 litre/2 pints red wine
2 cloves • 2 bay leaves
5ml/1tsp chopped parsley
5ml/1tsp fresh rosemary
10ml/2tsp wine vinegar

Make the marinade first. Mix together all the marinade ingredients. Put in the hare and leave overnight.

Remove the hare and dry it thoroughly. Strain the marinade and reserve the liquid. Cut the hare into small pieces. Cut the gammon into 2.5-cm/1-inch cubes. Melt the butter in a deep flameproof casserole or pot, add the cubed gammon and fry gently until well browned. Remove the cubed meat, put in the hare pieces and fry until browned on all sides. Sprinkle with the flour and cook for 2 minutes, stirring all the time. Add the marinade liquid. Add the garlic clove with the bouquet garni, sugar, salt and pepper. Return the gammon to the casserole, cover it and simmer gently for 2 hours. Add the onions, cook for 10 minutes longer, then add the mushrooms including their stalks. Cook for 15 minutes. Chop the hare's liver very finely or pound it until almost smooth. Stir the liver and the hare's blood into the civet, reduce the heat and steam for 3–4 minutes until the sauce thickens slightly. Remove the bouquet garni.

<u>SERVES 4</u>

Hasenrücken

This recipe gives the traditional German method for stewing a saddle of hare. The resulting dish is rich and wholesome – a perfect winter's meal.

1 large young hare
3 juniper berries
salt and pepper
150g/5oz bacon for larding
1 carrot
1 celery stick
100g/4oz butter or lard
½ onion, finely chopped
15ml/1tbsp chopped parsley
15ml/1tbsp flour
200ml/6fl oz boiling water or beef stock
150ml/¼ pint red wine
250ml/8fl oz double cream
20 peppercorns
10 allspice berries
1 bay leaf
pinch of dried thyme
2.5ml/½ tsp freshly grated nutmeg
pinch of ground ginger
juice of 1 lemon
30ml/2tbsp wine vinegar
15ml/1tbsp redcurrant or cranberry juice

Prepare the hare. Cut away the rib-cage, remove the legs and keep for another dish. Wash and dry the saddle well. Crush the juniper berries. Rub the hare all over with the juniper berries, salt and pepper. Lard with the bacon.

Chop the carrot and celery into 1- cm/½- inch pieces. Melt the butter or lard in a deep, heavy casserole, and fry the vegetables lightly with the parsley. Remove the vegetables.

Lay the larded hare in the pan, turning and basting until browned on all sides to seal in the juices. When the hare is well browned, lift it out of the pan. Return the vegetables, sprinkle in the flour and blend well with the juices. Pour on the boiling water or stock slowly, stirring to prevent lumps forming, then add the wine and cream. Add all the spices and herbs, the lemon juice, vinegar and the redcurrant or cranberry juice. Return the hare to the sauce and cover the pan closely. Cook slowly, basting occasionally, for about 1 hour until the meat is tender.

SERVES 5 TO 6

Haricot of Hare

Illustrated on page 98

Haricot, as well as being the name used for certain dried beans, is a term used for a rich stew, usually of lamb.

1 hare
45ml/3tbsp butter
100g/4oz onions, chopped
100g/4oz turnips, diced
225g/8oz carrots, diced
salt and pepper
15ml/1tbsp chopped parsley
2.5ml/½ tsp dried thyme
1 litre/2 pints All-purpose Stock (page 40)

Joint the hare. Melt the butter in a saucepan and fry the joints until well browned on all sides. Add the vegetables to the hare with the seasoning, herbs and stock. Cover tightly and stew gently for 2½–3 hours. Check the seasoning at the end of the cooking time.

SERVES 5 TO 6

Curried Rabbit

1 rabbit
50g/2oz butter
1 small onion, chopped
10ml/2tsp flour
15ml/1tbsp curry powder
10ml/2tsp curry paste
10ml/2tsp desiccated coconut
450ml/¾ pint chicken stock
1 apple, peeled, cored and chopped
10ml/2tsp mango chutney
15ml/1tbsp lemon juice
salt and pepper
25g/1oz sultanas
25g/1oz blanched almonds
30ml/2tbsp single cream or top of milk (optional)

GARNISH
paprika
lemon wedges

Joint the rabbit. Heat the butter in a saucepan and fry the joints lightly. Remove the meat and drain it. Fry the onion lightly in the same fat. Add the flour, curry powder and paste and continue frying, stirring occasionally, for 3–4 minutes. Tie the coconut in a piece of muslin. Stir the stock into the pan and bring to the boil. Put in all the other ingredients except the cream or milk, and lay the rabbit joints on top. Simmer for 15 minutes, then remove the coconut. Simmer gently for a further 1½ hours, adding a little extra stock if necessary. Stir in the cream or milk, if used. Remove the rabbit to a heated serving dish. Pour the sauce over it. Sprinkle lightly with paprika and garnish with lemon wedges.

Serve with rice cooked with whole spices.

SERVES 3 TO 4

Top: Casserole of Rabbit with Apples and Prunes (overleaf); Below: Curried Rabbit

Casserole of Rabbit with Apples and Prunes

Illustrated on previous page

1 rabbit
salt and pepper
60ml/4tbsp flour
65g/2½ oz butter
1 onion, sliced
225g/8oz cooking apples, peeled, cored and sliced
1 (213g/7½ oz) can prunes
1 chicken stock cube

GARNISH
chopped parsley
crescents of fried bread

Set the oven at 350°F/180°C/gas 4. Joint the rabbit and discard the lower forelegs and rib-cage, or keep for stock. Season half the flour lightly with salt and pepper and coat the rabbit lightly. Melt 50g/2oz of the butter in a flameproof casserole or frying pan, add the rabbit, and brown lightly on all sides. Remove the joints to a plate. Fry the onion in the butter until soft but not brown. Add the apples to the onion. Drain the prunes and make the juice up to 250ml/8fl oz with water. Add the stock cube, crumbling it finely. Return the rabbit to the casserole with the prunes and stock. Cover and cook for 1½ hours, or until the rabbit is tender.

When the rabbit is cooked, arrange the joints on a warmed serving dish with the apples and prunes; keep hot. Blend the remaining butter and flour together on a plate to make a beurre manié and add in small pieces to the liquid in the casserole. Bring to the boil and stir all the time until the sauce thickens. Check the seasoning before pouring the sauce over the rabbit. Sprinkle with chopped parsley. Surround with the crescents of fried bread and serve at once.

SERVES 4

Scotch Rabbit

This long-simmered dish is quite light and low in fat, particulary if lean cooked ham is substituted for the pork or bacon. Serve crunchy-skinned baked potatoes as an accompaniment, with some lightly steamed carrots and leeks, combined before cooking

1 rabbit
100g/4oz pork or *bacon*
1 cabbage
salt and pepper
2 tomatoes
1 small onion, chopped
1 bouquet garni
extra piece of pork or *bacon (optional)*
about 300ml/½ pint chicken stock

Cut the flesh from the rabbit bones (these can be used to make stock). Chop the rabbit meat and the pork or bacon, then mix together. Blanch the cabbage leaves and season them. Line a saucepan with some of the cabbage leaves.

Peel and chop the tomatoes. Put the meat, tomato, onion, seasoning and bouquet garni into the lined pan. Cover closely with more cabbage leaves and put the extra piece of pork or bacon on top, if liked. Heat enough stock in a separate pan to cover the cabbage. Bring to boiling point and pour it into the saucepan. Cover tightly and simmer for about 2½ hours, adding more stock if necessary. Remove the bouquet garni, check the seasoning and serve.

S E R V E S   4

Braised Rabbit in Beer

Light beer is used to cook the rabbit. Do not use a dark ale as it will overpower the flavour of the stew.

1 rabbit
salt and pepper
45ml/3tbsp flour
50g/2oz butter or *margarine*
15ml/1tbsp oil
1 large onion, chopped
100g/4oz rindless streaky bacon
100g/4oz button mushrooms
10ml/2tsp prepared English mustard
10ml/2tsp prepared French mustard
about 250ml/8fl oz lager
sugar (optional)
chopped parsley to garnish

Joint the rabbit. Soak the joints in a bowl of cold water for 30 minutes, then dry them thoroughly. Season the flour with salt and pepper. Coat the joints lightly with the seasoned flour, shake off the excess and put the unused flour to one side.

Set the oven at 350°F/180°C/gas 4. Heat half the butter or margarine in a frying pan, add the oil and fry the rabbit lightly. Remove, drain off any excess fat and place in a casserole. Add the onion to the pan, and cook very gently, without browning, for 10 minutes. Chop the bacon and add to the onion. Quarter the mushrooms, if large, and add them to the pan with both mustards and the lager. Season to taste. Spoon the mixture over the rabbit in the casserole. Cover the casserole and cook for 1½ hours, or until the rabbit is tender. The exact cooking time will vary, depending on the age and size of the animal.

When the rabbit is cooked, strain off the liquor from the casserole into a saucepan, bring to the boil and boil rapidly to reduce it by one-third.

Remove from the heat. Blend the remaining flour and butter together on a plate to make a beurre manié and add in small pieces to the saucepan. Stir well, return to the heat, and bring to the boil. Cook for 2 minutes to thicken and clear the sauce. Check and adjust the seasoning. If liked, add a little sugar to remove any bitterness from the lager. Pour the sauce over the rabbit and serve sprinkled with a little chopped parsley.

SERVES 4 TO 5

Hunter's Rabbit Casserole

A casserole which has an excellent flavour, why not serve cooked beans or pasta as an accompaniment? Toss cooked haricot or flageolet beans with butter, pepper and chopped parsley. Simply add a little butter to freshly cooked noodles if they are the accompaniment.

100g/4oz rindless rashers streaky bacon
900g/2lb rabbit joints
3 onions, sliced
2 carrots, sliced
2.5ml/½ tsp dried mixed herbs
salt and pepper
600ml/1pint chicken stock

Set the oven at 325°F/170°C/gas 3. Trim the bacon, and cut each rasher into three pieces. Layer the rabbit, bacon, and vegetables in a casserole, sprinkle with herbs and seasoning, then pour in the stock. Cover and cook for 1½–2 hours, or until the rabbit it tender.

SERVES 4

Rabbit Fricassée

A fricassée is a white stew, flavoured only with pale ingredients such as mushrooms. The cooking liquid is usually a white stock or milk as in this recipe.

450g/1lb boneless rabbit
1 small onion, finely chopped
salt and pepper
1 bay leaf
1 small blade of mace
100g/4oz small button mushrooms, sliced
about 250ml/8fl oz milk
5ml/1tsp cornflour
chopped parsley to garnish

Set the oven at 375°F/190°C/gas 5. Cut the rabbit into small pieces. Place them in a casserole. Add the onion with the seasoning, bayleaf and mace. Sprinkle in the mushrooms. Three-quarters fill the dish with milk, cover, and cook for 1–1¼ hours.

Blend the cornflour with a little cold milk and add to the liquid in the casserole, stirring all the time. Bring to the boil and cook for another 10 minutes. Sprinkle with chopped parsley before serving.

SERVES 3 TO 4

Rabbit Jardinière

The vegetables can be varied to taste in this casserole. Combine fresh root vegetables with beans or peas, using frozen varieties when they are out of season.

1 rabbit
1 onion, chopped
1 carrot, diced
½ turnip, diced
2 celery sticks, sliced
1 bouquet garni
6 peppercorns
5ml/1tsp salt
Onion Sauce (page 164)

GARNISH
chopped parsley
grilled bacon rolls (optional)

Truss the rabbit and put it into boiling, lightly salted water. When the water comes to the boil, add the vegetables together with the bouquet garni, peppercorns and salt. Poach gently for 45–60 minutes, until the rabbit is tender.

Meanwhile, heat the sauce. When the rabbit is tender, remove the skewers. Drain the rabbit. (Keep the cooking liquid for stock or broth.)

Lay the rabbit on a hot dish and pour the hot sauce over it. Serve very hot, sprinkled with the chopped parsley. Serve any extra sauce separately.

Garnish, if liked, with bacon rolls.

SERVES 4

Piquant Tomato Rabbit

50g/2oz dripping
4 rabbit joints
about 450ml/³⁄4 pint chicken stock
40g/1¹⁄2 oz butter
25g/1oz flour
200ml/7fl oz fresh tomato purée
grated rind of 1 lemon
salt and pepper
pinch of caster sugar
15ml/1tbsp fresh lemon juice

Melt the dripping in a saucepan and fry the pieces of rabbit until well browned on all sides. Drain off any surplus fat. Add enough stock just to cover the rabbit, cover with a tight-fitting lid and cook for about 1–1¼ hours, or until tender.

Meanwhile, melt the butter in a small saucepan, stir in the flour and cook gently until the roux is nut-brown, then stir in the tomato purée and lemon rind.

When the rabbit is cooked, remove it from the pan, drain and keep hot. Strain the stock and stir it into the tomato mixture. Stir until boiling. Season to taste, then add a pinch of sugar and the lemon juice. Put the rabbit joints in the sauce, heat thoroughly and serve at once.

S E R V E S   4

MRS BEETON'S TIP

Fine strips of lemon rind can be cooked in a little simmering water until tender, then drained and dried on absorbent kitchen paper. Sprinkle them over just before it is served.

Top: Civet of Venison (page 114); Below: Piquant Tomato Rabbit

Bigos

There are many ways of preparing what is in effect Poland's national dish. The essence of all of them is that they should consist of a mixture of sauerkraut and smoked sausage and the game secured by the hunter. Duck or any type of game can be used instead of venison.

1kg/2lb sauerkraut
450g/1lb boneless shoulder of venison
150g/5oz smoked pork sausages
50g/2oz lard
1 large onion, sliced
15ml/1tbsp flour
30ml/2 tbsp concentrated tomato purée
75ml/3fl oz vodka
75ml/3fl oz medium-dry white wine
salt and pepper
1 large green apple, peeled and cored
250ml/8fl oz chicken or beef stock
25g/1oz butter

Place the sauerkraut in a sieve or colander and rinse in cold water to wash off the vinegar. Put into a saucepan with enough water to cover and simmer for 20–30 minutes, until tender. Drain and put to one side.

Wipe the venison, trim off all fat and cut into 2.5 cm/1 inch cubes. Slice the sausages into pieces 1 cm/½ inch thick. Melt half the lard in a large frying pan and brown the onion until golden. Add a little of the flour and stir until the mixture is totally blended. Stir in the tomato purée, then the vodka and the wine. Reduce the heat and simmer for 5 minutes. Add all the meats, season to taste and mix together well. Cover with a tight-fitting lid and cook for 1 hour over a low heat, until the meats are tender.

Set the oven at 350°F/180°C/gas 4. Cut the apple into 3–4cm/1½-inch cubes. Put a bed of half the sauerkraut in a large ovenproof dish, followed by a layer of all the meats. Sprinkle with the apple cubes and place a final layer of the remaining sauerkraut on top. Heat the stock and pour half of it over the sauerkraut. Dot with flakes of butter and cook the bigos for about 2 hours.

About 10 minutes before the end of cooking time, melt the remaining lard in a frying pan, add the rest of the flour and stir over a low heat for 2–3 minutes, without allowing the mixture to colour. Draw the pan off the heat and gradually add the remaining stock, stirring all the time. Return to a moderate heat and stir well until the sauce (roux) thickens and is boiling. Simmer for 1–2 minutes, beating briskly. Season to taste.

Pour the roux over the sauerkraut and blend well. Return the dish to the oven and cook uncovered for a further 30 minutes, until the top is crisp and golden-brown. Serve very hot.

SERVES 4

Collared Venison

about 100ml/4fl oz port (optional)
8 thin slices lamb or pork fat
shoulder of venison
salt and pepper
750ml/1¼ pints Game Stock (page 40)
2.5ml/½ tsp black peppercorns
2.5ml/½ tsp ground allspice
Forcemeat Balls (page 172) to garnish

If port is used, soak the lamb or pork fat in it for 2–3 hours. Bone the venison, flatten it with a wooden mallet and season well. Cover with the slices of lamb or pork fat. Roll it up tightly and tie securely with tape. Bring the stock to simmering point in a large, heavy saucepan and add the meat with the venison bones, peppercorns, allspice and the port in which the fat was soaked. Simmer gently with a lid on the pan for 3–3½ hours.

Serve garnished with Forcemeat Balls and offer redcurrant jelly separately.

SERVES 10 TO 12

Civet of Venison

Illustrated on page 111

700g/1½ lb pieces or trimmings of stewing venison
Cooked Red Wine Marinade (page 170)
30ml/2tbsp oil
100g/4oz rindless rashers streaky bacon
100g/4oz button mushrooms
15ml/1tbsp concentrated tomato purée
25g/1oz butter
25g/1oz plain flour
salt and pepper
5ml/1tsp sugar
croûtons of fried bread to garnish

Place the venison in a bowl, cover with the marinade and leave for 24 hours. Drain the meat and reserve the marinade. Dry the meat well on absorbent kitchen paper.

Heat half the oil in a saucepan. Cut the bacon rashers into small pieces. Add to the saucepan with the mushrooms and cook for a few minutes until the bacon is lightly browned. Remove the bacon and mushrooms with a perforated spoon; put to one side. Add the remaining oil to the pan and heat it. Add the meat and cook fairly quickly to brown it all over. Return the bacon and mushrooms to the saucepan. Add the marinade, stir in the tomato purée, cover with a lid and simmer gently for 2–2½ hours, until the meat is tender.

Meanwhile, soften the butter and blend together with the flour to make a beurre manié. Off the heat, add this to the stew in small pieces. Return to the heat and stir until the beurre manié melts and the stew thickens. Add salt, pepper and sugar to taste. Garnish with croûtons of fried bread. Serve with boiled rice.

SERVES 4 TO 6

BRAISED AND
POACHED GAME

Poached Game Fillets

This is an excellant method of cooking tender pieces of boneless game.
Pheasant, duck or fine fillets of tender rabbit can also be used in the recipe.

2 young blackcock or *grouse*
1 onion, sliced
1 small carrot, sliced
½ turnip, sliced
3 rashers rindless streaky bacon
100ml/4floz Game Stock (page 40)
300ml/½ pint Foundation Brown Sauce (page 160)
butter for frying
12 button mushrooms
about 75ml/3floz sherry or *Madeira (optional)*
salt and pepper

Joint the birds and cut the meat into fillets; reserve the bones for making
stock. Place the vegetables in a sauté or frying pan with the bacon, then put
the fillets on top. Add the stock, cover with a buttered paper and a tight-
fitting lid and simmer gently for 30 minutes.

Meanwhile, heat the brown sauce. Melt the butter, fry the mushrooms
and keep them hot. Add the wine to the sauce, if used. Season to taste and
keep the sauce hot.

When the fillets are cooked, arrange them on a hot dish, strain the sauce
over them and use the cooked vegetables, mushrooms and bacon as a
garnish.

SERVES 5 TO 6

MRS BEETON'S TIP

*If you have bones for making stock but do not want to cook them immediately,
then freeze them until you have the time to boil them. The bones can be placed
in a pan, straight from the freezer, and cooked from frozen.*

Highland Grouse

Illustrated on page 119

The availability of frozen raspberries allows for this dish to be prepared while grouse is in season – even if the season for fresh fruit is long finished.

50g/2oz butter
2 young grouse
salt and pepper
225g/8oz raspberries
grated rind of 1 lemon

GARNISH
whole raspberries (optional)
herb sprigs or *watercress*

Set the oven at 400°F/200°C/gas 6. Place half the butter inside each bird and sprinkle well with salt and pepper. Mix the raspberries and lemon rind together and fill the cavities in the birds with the mixture. Put 5mm/¼ inch water in a deep overproof dish with a lid which will just hold the birds. Place the birds and any remaining raspberry mixture in the dish, and cover. Cook for 35–45 minutes. Remove the lid and cook for a further 10 minutes, to brown the birds.

Serve with creamed potatoes and a green vegetable. Garnish with a few whole raspberries and herb sprigs or watercress.

SERVES 4

Pigeons with Olives

Tangy stuffed green olives complement pigeons which are braised in a rich sauce. Serve buttered pasta or rice to accompany this dish.

3 woodpigeons
50g/2oz butter
600ml/1pint Espagnole Sauce (page 162)
24 stuffed green olives

Split each pigeon into quarters. Heat the butter and fry the pigeon quarters until well browned on all sides. Heat the Espagnole Sauce to simmering point in a flameproof casserole. Put the birds into the hot Espagnole Sauce, cover and simmer for about 45 minutes, or until they are cooked and tender.

Add the olives and cook for 4–5 minutes to heat them through. Serve the pigeons with the sauce and olives poured over them.

SERVES 6

Top: Highland Grouse (page 117); Below: Pigeons with Olives

Mrs Beeton's Hashed Partridges

Illustrated on page 122

This is an excellent recipe to use for grouse or pheasant as
well as for partridge.

3 cooked partridges
25g/1oz butter
oil for frying
25g/1oz sliced ham, diced
75g/3oz carrots, thinly sliced
50g/2oz mild onion or shallots, thinly sliced
25g/1oz button mushrooms
350ml/12fl oz Game Stock (page 40)
1 bouquet garni
4 whole cloves
4 black peppercorns
100ml/4fl oz medium-dry sherry or Madeira
1 lump of sugar (if using sherry)
fried bread croûtons to garnish

Joint the birds. Skin the wings, legs and breasts; keep the skin and carcasses.
Heat the butter and a little oil in a large, heavy pan, and fry the ham and
vegetables gently for 6–8 minutes, until softened but not browned. Add
the stock and bouquet garni. Tie the spices in muslin and add them, with
the skin and carcasses. Simmer for 15 minutes. Strain the sauce, then cool
and chill it.

When cold, take off all the fat. Add the wine and sugar, if used. Return to
the pan with the joints. Heat thoroughly to boiling point, then turn into a
heated serving dish. Scatter the croûtons over the dish and serve very hot.

SERVES 3 TO 4

Spanish Braised Partridge

Illustrated overleaf

A full-flavoured dish, laden with garlic and enriched with dark, plain chocolate. Dark, bitter chocolate is used to enrich savoury dishes without contributing any sweetness or clash of flavour.

2 partridges (about 450g/1lb each)
1 onion, chopped
1 clove
6 large garlic cloves
1 bay leaf
45ml/3 tbsp olive oil
150ml/¼ pint dry white wine
45ml/3tbsp white wine vinegar
salt and pepper
25g/1oz plain chocolate

GARNISH

sautéed potato slices
parsley sprigs

Put the partridges into a large, heavy saucepan. Add the onion to the pan. Stick the clove into one garlic clove and add to the pan with the remaining garlic, bay leaf, olive oil, wine, vinegar and a little salt and pepper. Bring to the boil, reduce the heat, then simmer for 35 minutes, shaking the pan well at intervals. Remove the partridges and keep hot on a serving dish.

Grate the chocolate, stir it into the pan and simmer for a further 10 minutes. Arrange some sliced, sautéed potatoes around the partridges. Rub the chocolate sauce through a sieve and pour it over them. Add a sprig or two of parsley to complete the garnish.

SERVES 4

Top: Hashed Partridges (page 120); Below: Spanish Braised Partridge (previous page)

Braised Duck

Since the skin of a duck is fatty, it is often open-roasted in a hot oven instead of being sealed in fat as the first stage in braising.

1 duck
2 onions, sliced
2 sage leaves
1 bouquet garni
600ml/1 pint All-purpose Stock (page 40)
40g/1½ oz butter
40g/1½ oz flour
salt and pepper
100g/4oz sliced mushrooms (optional)

Set the oven at 425°F/220°C/gas 7. Truss the duck and roast it for 20 minutes in the oven. Prick the skin all over and drain off all the fat from the bird. Place the duck in a saucepan with the onions, sage and bouquet garni. Pour in half the stock and heat it until it is just boiling. Cover tightly and cook slowly for 45 minutes, or until the duck is quite tender.

Melt the butter in a saucepan, add the flour and brown well, then gradually stir in the remaining stock and the cooking liquid from the duck. Simmer for 20 minutes, then strain.

Remove the trussing string from the duck. Season the sauce and serve in a sauceboat. Some mushrooms may be added to the sauce, if liked, and simmered for 5 minutes before serving.

S E R V E S   4   T O   5

Braised Stuffed Duck

50g/2oz butter
1 large duck
20ml/4tsp chopped shallot
15ml/1tbsp flour
300ml/½ pint All-purpose Stock (page 40)
about 100ml/4fl oz claret (optional)
1 bouquet garni
lemon juice

STUFFING

duck's heart and liver or 100g/4oz duck livers
1 small onion
25g/1oz butter
50g/2oz soft white breadcrumbs
5ml/1tsp chopped parsley
salt and pepper

Prepare the stuffing first. Chop the liver and heart finely. Parboil the onion and chop it finely. Melt the butter and add to the liver and heart with the onion, breadcrumbs, parsley and seasoning. Stuff the duck with this mixture, then truss it.

Set the oven at 350°F/180°C/gas 4. Melt the butter and fry the duck in a deep flameproof casserole with the chopped shallot until brown. Remove the duck. Stir the flour into the butter and brown it. Stir in the stock gradually, bring to boiling point, and add the claret, if used. Replace the duck in the pan and add the bouquet garni and lemon juice to taste. Cover with a tight-fitting lid. Cook for 1–1½ hours, or until the duck is tender. Remove the trussing string and joint the duck. Arrange it on a warmed serving dish and pour the sauce over it.

SERVES 4 TO 5

Braised Duck with Turnips

50g/2oz butter
1 duck
1 bouquet garni
6 black peppercorns
2 cloves
about 1.15 litres/2 pints All-purpose Stock (page 40)
3 young turnips, diced
about 75ml/3fl oz medium-dry sherry (optional)
salt and pepper

MIREPOIX
2 onions, sliced
1 small turnip, sliced
2 carrots, sliced
1 celery stick, sliced

Put the vegetables for the mirepoix in a large saucepan with the butter. Lay the duck on the vegetables and cover the pan. Fry gently for 20 minutes, then add the bouquet garni, spices and enough stock to cover three-quarters of the mirepoix. Cover closely and simmer gently for about 2 hours, or until the duck is tender. Add more stock if necessary during cooking to prevent it buring.

Meanwhile, boil the turnips in 600ml/1 pint of the remaining stock until tender. Drain, keep them hot and strain the stock from the duck and add it to the turnip stock. Boil it quickly until reduced by half. Add the sherry, if used, and season to taste. Serve the duck on a hot dish with turnips and mirepoix vegetables piled at either end. Serve the sauce separately.

SERVES 4 TO 5

Braised Rabbit with Rice

450g/1lb boneless rabbit
600ml/1pint All-purpose Stock (page 40)
225g/8oz long-grain rice
50g/2oz sultanas
25g/1oz butter
1 small onion, chopped
2 celery sticks, finely sliced
100g/4oz rindless streaky bacon
1 green pepper
salt and pepper

GARNISH

paprika
celery leaves

Cut the rabbit into serving portions, place in a saucepan with the stock and cook gently for about 40 minutes, until tender. Remove with a perforated spoon and put to one side.

Bring the stock to the boil, add the rice and sultanas and cook for 12–15 minutes, until the rice is tender. The rice should have absorbed almost all the liquid when cooked; add a little more stock if necessary.

Melt the butter in a large pan, add the onion and celery and cook gently until soft. Cut the bacon into pieces and add to the onion and celery. Cook for a few minutes until crisp. Halve the pepper and remove the seeds and pith. Cut the flesh into shreds and add it to the onion, celery and bacon. Cook for 5 minutes.

Stir the rice and sultanas into the onion, celery and bacon mixture with the rabbit. Heat gently but thoroughly. Add salt and pepper to taste. Place in a warmed dish, sprinkle with a little paprika and garnish with celery leaves.

SERVES 4 TO 5

Top: Farmer's Braised Rabbit (overleaf); Below: Braised Rabbit with Rice

Farmer's Braised Rabbit

Illustrated on previous page

In some versions of this old dish, beer or tea is used instead of wine or cider.

1 large rabbit with liver, heart and kidneys of the rabbit
8 prunes
600ml/1pint dry red, white or *rosé wine* or *dry cider*
flour for coating
45ml/3tbsp cooking oil
1 small onion, diced
150g/5oz carrots, diced
2 celery sticks, sliced
2 cloves garlic, finely chopped
25g/1oz concentrated tomato purée
1 bouquet garni
salt and freshly ground black pepper
pinch of ground mace
8 olives, green or *black*
8 button mushrooms
8 button or *pickling onions*
30ml/2tbsp cornflour • 100ml/4fl oz water

Keep the liver, heart, and kidneys to one side. Soak the rabbit in cold water for 1 hour to whiten the flesh. Steep the prunes in the wine or cider.

Dry the rabbit thoroughly. Cut it into eight serving portions and toss them lightly in the flour. Heat the oil in a large frying pan and fry the meat until the pieces are golden-brown all over, turning them as required. Transfer them to a heavy, ovenproof casserole. Keep the remaining oil.

Set the oven at 350°F/180°C/gas 4. Fry the vegetables gently in the oil, turning them over to brown them slightly. Add them to the casserole with the tomato purée, bouquet garni, seasoning and mace. Chop the liver, heart, and kidneys and add them to the casserole. Stone and add the olives. Stone the soaked prunes and add them with the liquid they have soaked in. Cover the casserole tightly, and cook for 1½ hours.

Meanwhile, sauté the button mushrooms in the frying pan. Boil the onions for 5 minutes in lightly salted water. Add both to the casserole 5 minutes before the end of the cooking time.

When the meat is done, strain the cooking liquid into a small saucepan, and remove the bouquet garni. Cover the casserole and keep hot. Blend the cornflour and water, stir into the cooking liquid and heat gently, stirring, until thickened. Check seasoning. Pour the sauce over the meat and serve.

SERVES 8

Rabbit Creole

450g/1lb boneless rabbit
1 small green pepper
1 (397g/14oz) can tomatoes
25g/1oz unsalted butter
15ml/1tbsp oil
1 onion, sliced
1 garlic clove, crushed
5ml/1tsp sugar
15ml/1tbsp concentrated tomato purée
salt • 2.5ml/½ tsp Tabasco sauce
10 stuffed olives

Cut the rabbit meat into small strips. Halve the pepper, remove the pith and seeds and slice it. Drain and cut up the tomatoes roughly. Put the butter and oil in a saucepan with the onion, garlic and pepper, then fry for 2–3 minutes without colouring. Add the rabbit and cook gently for 15 minutes, until the onion is soft, taking care not to brown it. Stir in all the remaining ingredients, cover and simmer gently for 25 minutes.

Serve with plain boiled rice or rice flavoured with pounded saffron strands, added to the cooking water.

SERVES 4 TO 5

Top: Marinated Venison Steaks; Below: Orange-scented Braised Venison (overleaf)

Marinated Venison Steaks

4 slices venison (from haunch)
salt and freshly ground black pepper
25g/1oz flour
butter or dripping
1 small onion, chopped
6 – 8 juniper berries
150ml/¼ pint Game or All-purpose Stock (page 40)
chopped parsley to garnish

M A R I N A D E
about 300m/½ pint red wine
1 bouquet garni
6 peppercorns
4 slices onion
30ml/2 tbsp olive oil
10ml/2 tsp red wine vinegar

Make the marinade first. Boil together all the ingredients listed for 1 minute. Allow to cool completely. Lay the venison steaks in a shallow dish and pour the marinade over them. Leave overnight.

Set the oven at 350°F/180°C/gas 4. Take the venison out of the marinade and pat dry. Snip the edges of the slices with scissors to prevent curling. Season the flour with salt and pepper and rub it over both sides of the venison steaks. Heat the fat in a large flameproof pan or roasting tin until it hazes. Sear the steaks on both sides in the fat. Add the onion when searing the second side.

Crush the juniper berries. Pour off all but a film of fat. Sprinkle the steaks with the crushed juniper. Pour the stock and a little of the marinade round them, covering about 1cm/½ inch of the depth of the dish. Cover tightly with foil and bake for 30 minutes, or until the steaks are tender. Drain and serve sprinkled with chopped parsley.

Remove the grease from the stock and serve it as a sauce.

S E R V E S   6   T O   8

Orange-scented Braised Venison

Illustrated on previous page

1–1.25kg/2¾ lb haunch or *shoulder of venison*
Red Wine Marinade (page 171)
25g/1oz dripping
1 orange
All-purpose Stock (page 40)
30ml/2tbsp redcurrant jelly
salt and freshly ground black pepper
25g/1oz butter
25g/1oz flour

MIREPOIX

1 onion, thickly sliced
2 carrots, thickly sliced
2 celery sticks, thickly sliced

GARNISH

watercress sprigs
orange slices
Forcemeat Balls (page 172)

Place the venison in a deep dish. Cover with the red wine marinade and leave for about 12 hours or overnight, basting and turning occasionally. Dry on absorbent kitchen paper and trim if required. Reserve the marinade. Heat the dripping and brown the venison on all sides. Remove and keep on one side.

Set the oven at 375°F/190°C/gas 5. Fry the vegetables for the mirepoix for a few seconds in the hot dripping, then place in the bottom of a large casserole. Pare off a few thin strips of rind from the orange. Strain the marinade into the casserole. Add the rind and enough stock just to cover the vegetables. Place the venison on top, cover with a well-greased piece of greaseproof paper and cover with a lid. Cook for 1¼ hours.

When cooked, carve the meat into slices. Arrange on a heated serving dish and keep hot. Strain the liquor from the vegetables into a pan. Squeeze the orange and strain the juice into the pan. Add the redcurrant jelly, salt and pepper and bring to the boil, stirring to dissolve the jelly. Blend the butter and flour together on a plate to make a beurre manié. Remove the pan from the heat and add the beurre manié in small pieces; stir until blended in. Return the pan to the heat, bring to the boil and cook for 2–3 minutes, until the sauce thickens. Pour the sauce over the venison and serve hot, garnished with watercress, orange and Forcemeat Balls.

Serve with a purée of chestnuts or creamed celeriac.

SERVES 6 TO 8

Cumberland Hashed Venison

350g/12oz cold roast venison
450ml/1 pint All-purpose Stock (page 40)
50g/2oz butter
45ml/3tbsp flour
45–60ml/3–4tbsp port
grated rind and juice of 1 small orange
60–75ml/4–5tbsp redcurrant jelly
salt and pepper
croûtons of fried bread to garnish

Slice the meat neatly. Break up any bones and put them with any meat trimmings into the stock. Simmer the stock gently for 45 minutes, then strain it.

Melt the butter in a large saucepan or flameproof casserole and stir in the flour. Cook for 3–4 minutes, then stir in the strained stock. Continue to stir until the sauce comes to the boil. Put in the meat, port, orange rind and juice, and the redcurrant jelly. Bring once more to the boil and heat through thoroughly. Season to taste.

Serve at once, garnished with the croûtons. Offer extra redcurrant jelly separately.

SERVES 3 TO 4

Poached Rabbit Portions in Cream Sauce

3 – 4 parsley sprigs
1 bay leaf
1 blade of mace
2 rabbit joints
½ small onion, sliced
1 small carrot, sliced
salt and pepper
15ml/1 tbsp butter or margarine
15ml/1tbsp flour
butter for greasing
pinch of ground allspice
1 egg yolk
30ml/2tbsp single cream
a few drops of lemon juice

Tie the parsley sprigs, bay leaf, and mace in a small piece of muslin. Put the rabbit joints in a small, heavy saucepan, cover with water and bring slowly to the boil. Skim well. Add the vegetables and the muslin bag, then season with salt. Simmer gently for 1 hour, or until the joints are tender. Meanwhile, melt the fat in a small pan, stir in the flour and cook gently for 3 minutes, stirring all the time. Put to one side.

Drain the meat and vegetables, discard the muslin bag and keep the meat and vegetables warm under buttered paper. Strain the cooking liquid, and reserve 300ml/½ pint of it. Return the roux to the heat and gradually stir in the measured liquid. Cook for 3 minutes, stirring all the time. Season to taste with salt, pepper and allspice.

Return the meat and vegetables to the sauce, reduce the heat, and simmer very gently for 5–7 minutes. Beat the egg yolk with the cream and stir into the sauce. Add a few drops of lemon juice. Continue cooking until thoroughly reheated, but do not boil. Serve immediately.

SERVES 2

PIES

Grouse Pie

Illustrated on page 95

A traditional-style game pie, filled with game on the bone. If you prefer, use four grouse but cut off the breasts only to put in the pie.

*2 grouse
350g/12oz rump steak
2 hard-boiled eggs
2–3 rashers rindless bacon
salt and pepper
250ml/8fl oz Game Stock (page 40)
flour for rolling out
225g/8oz prepared puff pastry, defrosted if frozen
beaten egg or milk for glazing*

Joint the birds. Slice the steak thinly and slice the eggs. Cut the bacon rashers into strips. Season the steak and eggs to taste. Line the bottom of a 1-litre/2-pints pie dish with some of the pieces of seasoned steak. Cover with a layer of grouse and pack round them some bacon, egg and seasoning. Repeat the layers until the dish is full. Add enough stock to fill three-quarters of the pie dish.

Set the oven at 425°F/220°C/gas 7. Roll out the pastry on a lightly floured surface to make a lid. Moisten the rim of the dish and fit on the lid. Trim, crimp the edge, and make a small hole in the centre to allow steam to escape. Decorate with the trimmings. Bake the pie for 20 minutes, then lower the heat to 350°F/180°C/gas 4 and cook for another 1¼–1½ hours. Glaze the pastry with the egg or milk 30 minutes before the cooking is complete.

Meanwhile, simmer the necks and trimmings of the birds in the remaining stock; strain and season. Pour the hot stock into the pie through the hole just before serving.

SERVES 6 TO 8

Pigeon Pie

2 pigeons
salt and pepper
45ml/3tbsp flour
45ml/3tbsp corn oil
100g/4oz chuck steak, cubed
100g/4oz button onions
30ml/2tbsp sage and onion stuffing mix
1 smalll cooking apple, peeled, cored and sliced
250ml/8fl oz beef stock
225g/8oz prepared puff pastry, defrosted if frozen
flour for rolling out
beaten egg for glazing

Cut the pigeons into quarters. Remove the feet and backbone. Season the flour with salt and pepper. Coat the pigeon joints with seasoned flour. Heat the oil and fry the joints in the oil for about 10 minutes, turning as required, until lightly browned all over.

Dip the steak in the seasoned flour. Remove the pigeons from the pan and drain on absorbent kitchen paper. Put the steak and onions in the pan and cook for 5 minutes, turning frequently.

Make up the stuffing according to the packet directions. Make into small balls and fry in the pan to brown them lightly all over. Remove and drain.

Set the oven at 425°F/220°C/gas 7. In a large casserole or pie dish, layer all the filling ingredients, adding salt and pepper to taste. Pour in the stock. Roll out the pastry on a lightly floured surface to fit the dish. Moisten the rim of the pie dish and cover the pie with the pastry. Brush the crust with the egg.

Cook for 20 minutes, until the pastry is risen and golden. Reduce the heat to 350°F/180°C/gas 4, and cook for a further 2 hours, or until the pigeons are tender when pierced with a skewer through the crust. Cover the pie crust with buttered paper if necessary to prevent it over-browning or drying out.

SERVES 4 TO 5

French Game Pie

1 blackcock or *cock pheasant* or *2 large partridges* or *2 – 3 pigeons*
salt and pepper
350g/12oz lean minced veal
350g/12oz lean minced pork
2.5ml/½ tsp dried mixed herbs
8 mushrooms, finely chopped
2–3 rashers rindless bacon, chopped
100ml/4fl oz Game Stock (page 40)
100g/4oz prepared puff pastry, defrosted if frozen
beaten egg or *milk for glazing*

STUFFING
2 small onions, thickly sliced
4 sage leaves or 2.5ml/½ tsp dried rubbed sage
100g/4oz soft white breadcrumbs
50g/2oz butter
1 egg (optional)

First make the stuffing. Place the onion in a saucepan with a little water and parboil. Drain and chop the onion finely. Scald the fresh sage leaves, if used, and chop finely. Mix together the sage, onion and breadcrumbs. Melt the butter and add to the stuffing. Season to taste. Beat the egg lightly and add sufficient to the stuffing to bind it. Form into small balls.

Cut the game into neat joints and season the pieces lightly. Mix together the veal, pork, herbs, salt, pepper and mushrooms.

Set the oven at 400°F/200°C/gas 6. Put a layer of minced meat in the bottom of a 1.5–litre/2½–pint pie dish, then a layer of game, and then one of bacon and the stuffing balls. Repeat these layers until the dish is full. Moisten with the stock.

Roll out the pastry on a lightly floured surface to make a lid for the dish. Moisten the rim of the dish and fit on the lid. Decorate with the trimmings. Glaze and bake for 30 minutes. Reduce the heat to 350°F/180°C/gas 4 and bake for a further 1–1¼ hours. Serve hot or cold.

SERVES 6 TO 8

Raised Pheasant Pie (overleaf)

Raised Pheasant Pie

Illustrated on previous page

450g/1lb plain flour
2.5ml/½ tsp salt
225g/8oz butter or margarine
2 egg yolks
about 150ml/¼ pint cold water
1 hen pheasant, boned with carcass (page 38)
freshly grated nutmeg
1.25ml/¼ tsp ground allspice
salt and pepper
2 quantities Basic Forcemeat (page 172)
2 veal escalopes
1 thick slice cooked ham (about 50–75g/2–3oz)
beaten egg to glaze
1 small onion, quartered • 1 bay leaf
1 carrot, quartered lengthways
10ml/2tsp gelatine

To make the pastry, mix the flour and salt in a large bowl, then add the butter or margarine and rub it into the flour until the mixture resembles fine breadcrumbs. Make a well in the middle and add the egg yolks with a little of the water. Mix the pastry to a smooth, fairly soft dough, adding extra water as necessary. The pastry should have a little more water than ordinary short crust dough but it must not be sticky.

Set the oven at 325°F/160°C/gas 3. Grease a 23-cm/9-inch raised pie mould with a little oil and place it on a baking sheet. Set aside one third of the pastry for the lid and decorations, then roll out the remainder into an oblong shape, about twice the size of the top of the mould. Do not be tempted to roll the pastry out into a sheet large enough to completely line the mould as it can break easily when you lift it into the mould. Carefully lift the pastry into the mould, then use the back of your fingers and knuckles to press it into the base of the mould, smoothing it up the sides to line the mould completely. Take plenty of time to ensure that the mould is well lined with pastry and that there are no breaks in the lining.

Open out the pheasant and sprinkle it with a little nutmeg, the allspice and some seasoning. Set aside half the forcemeat, then divide the remainder into two portions. Spread one portion over the middle of the pleasant and lay the veal escalopes on top. Lay the cooked ham on top of the veal, then spread the second portion of forcemeat over the ham. Fold the sides of the boned pheasant around the stuffing to enclose it completely.

Put half the reserved forcemeat into the bottom of the pie, particularly round the edges. Put the pheasant in the pie, placing the join in the skin downwards (there is no need to sew up the opening as the pie will keep the filling inside the bird). Use the remaining forcemeat to fill in round the pheasant, packing it neatly into all the gaps.

Cut off a small piece of the remaining pastry and set it aside to make leaves for decoration. Roll out the rest slightly larger than the top of the pie. Dampen the rim of the pastry lining with a little water, then lift the lid on top of the pie and press the edges to seal in the filling. Trim off any excess pastry – you may find that snipping it off with a pair of kitchen scissors is the easiest method. Pinch up the pastry edges. Roll out the trimmings with the reserved pastry and cut out leaves to decorate the top of the pie. Cut a small hole to allow steam to escape, then glaze the pie with beaten egg.

Bake the pie for 3 hours. Check the pie frequently and cover it loosely with a piece of foil after the first hour to prevent the pastry from overcooking. Increase the oven temperature to 375°F/190°C/gas 5, uncover the pie and glaze it with a little more egg. Cook for a further 20–30 minutes, until the pastry is golden and glossy.

While the pie is cooking, simmer the pheasant carcass with the onion, bay leaf and carrot for 1½ hours. Make sure that there is plenty of water in the saucepan to cover the carcass and keep the pan covered. Strain the stock, then boil it hard, uncovered, until it is reduced to 300ml/½ pint. Strain it through a muslin-lined sieve, then taste and season it.

When the pie is cooked, heat the stock and sprinkle the gelatine into it. Remove the pan from the heat and stir until the gelatine has dissolved completely. Set this aside to cool. When the pie has cooled until it is just hot and the stock is cold, pour the stock slowly in through the vent in top.

Leave the pie to cool in the tin, then carefully remove the clips which hold the sides of the tin together and ease the sides away from the pie. Have a small pointed knife to ease away any small pieces of pastry that are stuck.

SERVES 6 TO 8

Top: Macédoine of Vegetables (page 172); Below: Durham Rabbit Pie

Durham Rabbit Pie

225g/8oz cooked rabbit
50g/2oz rindless boiled bacon
4 eggs • salt and pepper
beaten egg or milk for glazing

SHORTCRUST PASTRY
225g/8oz plain flour
2.5ml/½ tsp salt
100g/4oz butter or margarine
about 45ml/3tbsp cold water
flour for rolling out

First make the pastry. Sift together the flour and salt into a bowl. Rub in the fat until the mixture resembles fine breadcrumbs. Mix to a stiff dough with the cold water. Roll out on a lightly floured surface and use half of it to line a 20-cm/8-inch pie dish or plate.

Set the oven at 400°F/200°C/gas 6. Chop the rabbit meat and bacon finely and mix together. Place the mixture on the pastry in the form of a cross, leaving the outside edge of the pastry uncovered. Break an egg carefully into each uncovered pastry triangle, taking care not to break the yolks. Season well. Dampen the edges of the pastry, cover with the remaining rolled-out pastry and glaze with egg or milk. Bake for 30 - 40 minutes. Serve hot as a supper dish.

SERVES 4

Rabbit Pie

Illustrated on page 163

450g/1lb boneless rabbit
1 small onion, chopped
salt and pepper
150ml/¼ pint water
30ml/2tbsp cornflour
45ml/3tbsp milk
30ml/2tbsp chopped parsley
2 hard-boiled eggs
milk for glazing

SHORTCRUST PASTRY

225g/8oz plain flour
100g/4oz butter or margarine
4.5ml/3tbsp cold water

Cut the rabbit into large pieces and place in a saucepan. Add the onion to the pan with salt, pepper and the water. Cover and simmer slowly for 1¼ hours, or until the rabbit is tender. Remove the rabbit meat. Blend the cornflour with the milk and stir into the rabbit stock. Bring slowly to the boil, stirring all the time, and cook until the sauce thickens and clears. Stir in the parsley and rabbit meat. Leave the sauce to cool.

Meanwhile, make the pastry. Sift together the flour and salt into a bowl and rub in the fat. Add just enough water to bind the pastry.

Set the oven at 425°F/220°C/gas 7. Roll out the pastry on a lightly floured surface, and use half of it to line a 23-cm/9-inch shallow pie plate. Arrange the rabbit mixture in the centre. Slice the hard-boiled eggs and place on top. Dampen the edges of the base pastry lightly with milk, cover with the remaining pastry, seal and crimp the edges. Glaze the top crust with milk and make a small hole in the centre. Cook the pie for 15 minutes, then reduce the heat to 375°F/190°C/gas 5 and bake for a further 25–30 minutes. Serve hot or cold.

SERVES 4 TO 5

Hare Pie

Illustrated on page 163

275g/10oz cooked hare
225g/8oz rindless streaky bacon or a piece of boiling bacon
100g/4oz soft white breadcrumbs
gravy or stock made from the bones
salt and pepper
dash of Worcestershire sauce
fat for greasing
450g/1lb creamed potato
25g/1oz butter

Cut the hare meat off the bone and cut it into small pieces. Cut the bacon into small squares or cubes, and fry gently until just tender. Mix with the pieces of hare, the breadcrumbs and just enough gravy or stock to moisten. Season, and add the Worcestershire sauce.

Set the oven at 425°F/220°C/gas 7. Place half the meat mixture in the bottom of a greased pie dish and cover with half the creamed potato. Repeat these two layers. Dot the top potato layer with the butter. Cook for 30 minutes, or until the top is golden brown.

Serve hot, with Cumberland Sauce (page 165) or Prune Sauce (page 169) and with sweet-sour pickles or chutney.

SERVES 4 TO 5

Pigeon or Rabbit Pudding

Illustrated on page 95

Light suet pastry encloses a flavoursome filling of game and steak. Perfect for winter dinners, serve simply cooked Brussels sprouts or other seasonal vegetables as an accompaniment.

3 woodpigeons or 1kg/2lb boneless rabbit meat
225g/8oz chuck steak
salt and pepper
25g/1oz flour
2 hard-boiled eggs
150ml/5fl oz All-purpose Stock (page 40)

SUET CRUST PASTRY

350g/12oz plain flour
2.5ml/½ tsp salt
5ml/1 tsp baking powder
50g/5oz shredded suet
about 200ml/7fl oz cold water

First make the pastry. Sift together the flour, salt and baking powder. Mix in the suet and enough water to make a firm dough.

Skin the pigeons, if used. Cut pigeons into quarters or rabbit meat into 6-cm/2½–inch pieces. Cut the steak into small pieces. Season the flour with salt and pepper to taste. Dip the pieces of meat in the seasoned flour. Cut the eggs into sections. Line a greased 1-litre/2-pint pudding basin with two-thirds of the suet crust pastry, then put in the prepared meat and eggs. Add the stock and cover with the remaining pastry. Cover with greased paper or foil. Steam the pudding for at least 3½ hours. Serve with thin gravy.

SERVES 6

PÂTÉS, TERRINES AND COLD PLATTERS

Potted Game

Good for picnics, a first course or for an elegant yet light lunch. Remember that a well-presented portion also makes an acceptable gift.

350g/12oz cooked boneless game meat
100g/4oz cooked ham or boiled bacon
100ml/4fl oz Game Stock (page 40) or 60ml/4tbsp butter
pinch of cayenne pepper
salt
1.25ml/¼ tsp ground black pepper
melted clarified butter

GARNISH

bay leaves
juniper berries

Trim off any skin and fat from the meat, and chop or mince very finely with the ham or bacon. Gradually adding the stock or butter, pound to make a smooth paste. Add the cayenne pepper and seasoning to taste. Turn into small pots and cover with clarified butter Garnish each pot with a bay leaf and juniper berries. Leave until the butter is firm.

MAKES ABOUT 450g / 1 lb

Terrine of Duck

Illustrated on page 167

This flavoursome terrine is good for lunch or supper. Serve crusty bread
and a full-bodied red wine as the accompaniments.

450g/1lb boneless duck meat
100ml/4fl oz brandy
225g/8oz fresh belly of pork
275g/10oz boneless chicken
2 shallots, chopped • rind of 1 orange
pinch each of dried thyme and savory
salt and pepper • 3 eggs, beaten
450g/1lb thin slices pork back fat or streaky bacon rashers
3 bay leaves to garnish

Use only fleshy meat and discard any sinewy fibres. Mince or shred the
duck meat finely. Put it into a bowl with the brandy and leave to marinate
for 4–6 hours.

Mince the pork and chicken meat. Mix them with the duck meat and
shallots in the bowl. Cut the orange rind into thin shreds and add with the
herbs and seasoning. Stir in the eggs and mix together thoroughly.

Set the oven at 350°F/180°C/gas 4. Line a 1.4 - litre/2½ - pints
ovenproof dish with slices of pork fat or bacon, reserving enough to cover
the top of the dish. Put in the meat mixture. Smooth and level the top and
arrange the bay leaves in a trefoil pattern in the centre. Cover with the
reserved slices of fat, then with foil. Stand the dish in a pan of hot water
which comes half-way up the sides of the dish. Bake for 1¼ hours, or until
the pâté shrinks slightly from the sides of the dish and any melted fat on the
top is clear. Remove the foil and fat 15 minutes before the end of the
cooking time to let the pâté brown slightly. When cooked, weight the
terrine and cool it. Chill for 12 hours. Serve, cut in slices, from the dish.

MAKES ABOUT 1.5 kg / 3 lb

Duck Salad

This salad makes a delicious light meal, served with warm crusty bread or with baked potatoes. Instead of mayonnaise you may prefer to use a low-fat fromage frais. Served in small, individual portions, this salad also makes a tempting first course.

1 cold roast duck
1 small celery heart
salt and pepper
45ml/3tbsp french dressing
1 lettuce
½ bunch watercress
mayonnaise as required
10ml/2tsp chopped parsley (optional)
10ml/2tsp chopped olives (optional)
2 slices unpeeled orange, halved, to garnish

Cut the duck into strips and slice the celery. Mix in a basin with the seasoning and two-thirds of the french dressing, and leave to stand. Line a flat salad platter with lettuce leaves and watercress sprigs, then spoon over the rest of the french dressing. Place the duck mixture in the centre of the platter and cover with a thin layer of mayonnaise. Sprinkle with the parsley and olives, if used. Garnish with the halved orange slices.

SERVES 6

Top: Duck Salad; Below: Potted Hare (page 158)

Jellied Game Salad

Illustrated on page 167

4 hard-boiled eggs
350g/12oz lean cooked ham
600ml/1 pint Aspic (page 160)
450g/1lb cold cooked game meat (bird or animal)
about ¼ cucumber, peeled and thinly sliced

Cut the eggs into round slices. Cut the ham into slices, then into rounds of the same size as the eggs.

Rinse a plain 1-litre/2-pint mould with cold water and line it with aspic. Decorate the base of the mould with some of the ham and all the egg sandwiched together. Pour a little cold liquid aspic over them and allow to set to a jelly. Cut the game meat into neat small pieces. Sandwich together the remaining ham and cucumber slices. Arrange pieces of seasoned game and rounds of ham and cucumber on the set jelly. Pour more aspic on top and allow this to set. Repeat the layers until the mould is full; chop and include any extra egg white from the ends of the eggs, if liked. Allow each layer of jelly to set firmly before adding the next layer of meat.

When the jelly has set firmly, unmould. Any remaining aspic can be chopped on a wet board and used for decoration.

SERVES 4

Rabbit Charlotte

If you like, enliven this simple charlotte by adding fresh herbs – some chopped parsley and a little thyme; chopped tarragon or a leaf or two of chopped sage with snipped chives.

4 large slices of bread
butter
350g/12oz boneless rabbit, finely chopped or minced
300ml/½ pint milk
2 eggs, beaten
salt and pepper
chopped parsley to garnish

Set the oven at 350°F/170°C/gas 3. Remove the crusts and butter the bread. Put half at the bottom of a pie dish with the buttered side uppermost. Cover with the chopped or minced meat. Place the remaining bread and butter on top, buttered side up.

Warm the milk. Mix the eggs with the warm milk and season well. Pour into the dish and stand it in a larger dish of hot water. Bake the cooked meat for 1¼–1½ hours. Garnish with chopped parsley.

S E R V E S 4

MRS BEETON'S TIP

Cooked leftover game can be used in this charlotte. It can be served in the same way as a terrine, cut into wedges. A light salad is adequate accompaniment.

Top: Marbled Rabbit; Below: Baked Hare Pâté (page 157)

Marbled Rabbit

2 rabbits
salt and pepper
450g/1lb pickled pork or boiling bacon
about 1.15 litres/2 pints chicken stock
2.5ml/½ tsp dried mixed herbs
5ml/1tsp chopped parsley
fresh white breadcrumbs (see method)
1 egg
fat for shallow frying
10ml/2tsp gelatine
2 hard-boiled eggs, sliced

Joint the rabbits, reserving the liver and kidneys. Leave the joints for at least 1 hour in strongly salted water. Slice the pork or bacon, then chop half of it finely. Keep the chopped portion aside. Pack the rabbit joints in a saucepan with the sliced pork or bacon on top and barely cover with stock. Cover tightly and simmer gently for 1¼–1½ hours, until the rabbit is tender.

Lift out the joints, drain them over the pan and remove the bones, leaving the flesh in large pieces. Trim into neat shapes. Chop the trimmings finely. Mix them with the herbs, seasoning and parsley, then weigh the mixture and add half its weight in breadcrumbs. Add some of the chopped pork or bacon and bind with egg. Mix thoroughly. Form into small balls and poach them for 10 minutes in the stock. Drain and put to one side. Fry first the livers and kidneys then the remaining pork or bacon in a little fat. Slice the livers and kidneys.

Strain 300ml/½ pint of the stock into a small bowl. Sprinkle the gelatine over it and then stand over a saucepan of hot water stirring until the gelatine has dissolved. Allow to cool but not set. Pour a little into a wetted mould and let it set. Cover with pieces of rabbit, layered with the remaining chopped pork or bacon, the forcemeat balls, slices of liver and kidney and slices of hard-boiled egg. Do not pack down tightly; fill up the mould with the remaining stock, covering the ingredients completely. Leave for 3–4 hours to set, then turn out.

SERVES 8

Steamed Rabbit Cream

This delicately set cream of rabbit can be served instead of a pâté as the first course of the meal. It is also suitable for lunch or supper; serve crisp, freshly made toast to offer a contrast in texture.

350g/12oz lightly cooked or raw rabbit
250ml/8fl oz milk
50g/2oz butter
45ml/3tbsp fresh white breadcrumbs
salt and pepper
150ml/¼ pint single cream
4 egg whites
fat for greasing

Mince or chop the rabbit finely. Heat the milk and butter together gently, until the butter melts. Add the breadcrumbs, rabbit and seasoning. Stir in the cream. Beat the egg white until stiff, and fold it in. Put into a greased mould or soufflé dish, and cover with greased paper or foil. Steam for about 45 minutes if using cooked meat, or for 1¼ hours for raw meat. The cream should be lightly set when cooked. Place on a warmed plate and serve with Fresh Tomato Sauce (page 168).

SERVES 4 TO 6

Baked Hare Pâté

Illustrated on page 154

Cut in small blocks, this pâté makes a good last-course savoury with a glass of Madeira or port. It is too rich for a first course.

450g/1lb cooked boneless hare meat
butter for frying
50g/2oz flat mushrooms, sliced
1 thick slice of white bread
15ml/1tbsp milk
50g/2oz slightly salted butter
2 egg yolks
60 – 90ml/4 – 6tbsp cooking brandy or *Marsala* or *Madeira*
a little gravy if necessary
salt and pepper
butter for greasing
1 bay leaf to garnish

Chop the meat. Melt a little butter in a pan and fry the mushrooms gently until softened. Remove the crust and soak the bread in the milk until well moistened, then mash thoroughly. Mix together the meat, mushrooms and bread, then mince or process in an electric blender. Add the butter, egg yolks and liquor, then mix together thoroughly. Moisten with a little gravy if necessary. Season to taste.

Set the oven at 325°F/170°C/gas 3. Grease a terrine or pie dish with butter. Put the bay leaf in the bottom, turn in the hare mixture and cover tightly. Stand the dish in a pan of hot water which comes half-way up the sides of the dish. Bake for 2 hours.

When cooked, weight the pâté and cool it. Chill for 12 hours. Turn out to serve, so that the bay leaf is on top of the pâté.

Serve in thin slices with rye bread and celery.

MAKES ABOUT 300G / 11OZ

Potted Hare

Illustrated on page 151

1 hare
4 rashers rindless streaky bacon
1 bouquet garni
6 juniper berries
1.25ml/¼ tsp ground cloves
1.25ml/¼ tsp ground mace
2 bay leaves
salt and freshly ground black pepper
pinch of cayenne pepper
Game Stock to cover (page 40)
melted clarified butter

GARNISH
4 bay leaves
juniper berries

Set the oven at 275°F/140°C/gas 1. Prepare the hare and cut into small neat pieces. Line the base of a casserole with the bacon rashers. Pack the pieces of hare closely on top, then add the herbs, spices and seasoning. Just cover with stock. Cover the casserole with a tight-fitting lid and cook for about 3 hours. Add more stock while cooking, if necessary.

When cooked, remove the meat from the bones, then chop and mince the meat together with the bacon. Moisten with a little of the stock and check the seasoning. Turn into four individual pots and cover with clarified butter. Garnish with bay leaves and juniper berries, then leave until the butter is firm.

MAKES ABOUT 800G / 1 ¾ LB

MRS BEETON'S TIP

When minced, the hare meat may weigh nearly 1kg/2lb. Since 450g/1lb potted hare is enough for 8 people, you may wish to pot the legs only.

ACCOMPANIMENTS

Aspic

1 quantity Game Stock or All-purpose Stock (pages 40)
salt and pepper
2 egg whites plus washed and crushed shells
15ml/3tsp gelatine

Prepare the stock and strain it through a muslin-lined sieve. Return it to the rinsed saucepan, bring it to the boil and boil hard until reduced to 600ml/1pint. Season, cool, then chill and remove fat.

Scald a piece of muslin and a sieve in boiling water. Heat the stock in a clean pan until it is just hot. Add the egg whites and the crushed shells, then whisk the stock over a low heat until it is quite frothy on the surface. Stop whisking and increase the heat, then allow the stock to come to the boil. As the froth rises to the top of the pan turn off the heat, or remove the pan from the heat, and allow it to subside. Boil the stock in this way two or three times, until the egg mixture has formed a firm crust and the stock is clear.

Strain the stock through the scalded muslin in the sieve, taking care to break up the crust of egg white as little as possible. The strained stock should be clear. Pour it back into the washed saucepan and heat gently until it is hot but not boiling. Add the gelatine and stir until it has dissolved completely. Use as required.

MAKES 600 ML / 1 PINT

Foundation Brown Sauce

25g/1oz dripping or lard
1 small carrot, sliced
1 onion, sliced
25g/1oz plain flour
600ml/1 pint All-purpose Stock (page 40)
salt and pepper

Melt the dripping or lard in a saucepan. Fry the carrot and onion slowly until the onion is golden-brown. Stir in the flour, reduce the heat and cook the flour very gently until it is also golden-brown. Draw the pan off the heat and gradually add the stock, stirring all the time to prevent lumps forming. Return to a moderate heat and stir the sauce until boiling. Reduce the heat, cover and simmer for 30 minutes. Strain the sauce. Season to taste.

M A K E S   A B O U T   3 0 0   M L / ½   P I N T

Bread Sauce

2 cloves
1 large onion
250ml/8fl oz milk
1 blade of mace
4 peppercorns
1 allspice berry
1 bay leaf
50g/2oz dried white breadcrumbs
15ml/1tbsp butter
salt and pepper
30ml/2tbsp single cream (optional)

Stick the cloves into the onion. Heat the milk very slowly to boiling point with the spices, bay leaf and studded onion. Reduce the heat, cover the pan and infuse the milk over a very gentle heat for 30 minutes.

Strain the flavoured liquid. Add the breadcrumbs and butter to the flavoured milk. Season to taste. Heat the mixture to just below simmering point and keep at this temperature for 20 minutes, stirring occasionally until nicely thickened. Stir in the cream, if used, just before serving.

M A K E S   A B O U T   2 5 0 M L / 8 F L O Z

Espagnole Sauce

50g/2oz lean raw ham or bacon
50g/2oz butter
1 small onion, sliced
1 small carrot, sliced
50g/2oz mushrooms, sliced
50g/2oz plain flour
600ml/1 pint All-purpose Stock (page 40)
1 bouquet garni
6 black peppercorns
1 bay leaf
150ml/¼ pint tomato pulp or 15ml/1tbsp concentrated tomato purée
salt
60ml/4tbsp sherry (optional)

Chop the ham or bacon into small pieces. Melt the butter in a saucepan and fry the ham or bacon for 2–3 minutes. Add the vegetables, and fry very slowly for 8–10 minutes, until golden-brown. Add the flour and stir until smooth. Cook over a gentle heat, stirring frequently, for about 10 minutes, or until the flour is a rich brown colour. Draw the pan off the heat and gradually add the stock, stirring all the time to prevent lumps forming. Add the bouquet garni, peppercorns and bay leaf. Return to a moderate heat and stir until boiling. Half cover the pan, reduce the heat and simmer the sauce gently for 30 minutes. Add the tomato pulp or concentrated tomato purée. Simmer the sauce for a further 30 minutes. Rub through a fine nylon sieve. Season to taste with salt. Add the sherry, if used. Reheat the sauce before serving.

MAKES 300–450ML/½–¾ PINT

Top: Rabbit Pie (page 144); Below: Hare Pie (page 145)

Velouté Sauce

50g/2oz butter
6 button mushrooms
12 black peppercorns
a few parsley sprigs
50g/2oz flour
600ml/1 pint All-purpose Stock (page 40)
salt and pepper
lemon juice
60 – 120ml/4 – 8tbsp single cream

Melt the butter in a saucepan and add the mushrooms, peppercorns and parsley. Cook gently for 10 minutes. Add the flour and stir over a gentle heat for 2–3 minutes, without allowing it to colour. Draw the pan off the heat and add the stock gradually, stirring well to prevent lumps forming. Return to a gentle heat and heat the sauce to simmering point, stirring all the time. Simmer for 3–4 minutes.

Rub the sauce through a sieve. Season to taste with salt and pepper, then add lemon juice to taste. Reheat the sauce to boiling point and stir in enough cream to give the desired flavour and consistency. Do not reboil the sauce. Use at once.

MAKES ABOUT 600 ML/1 PINT

Onion Sauce

2 onions, chopped
450ml/¾ pint water
40g/1½ oz butter or margarine
40g/1½ oz plain flour
300ml/½ pint milk
salt and pepper
a few drops of lemon juice

Put the onions in a saucepan and add the water. Bring to the boil, reduce the heat and simmer for 10–15 minutes, until softened. Drain thoroughly and reserve 300ml/½ pint of the cooking liquid to make the sauce.

Melt the butter in a saucepan and add the flour. Stir over a low heat for a couple of minutes, then gradually add the milk and reserved onion cooking liquid, stirring all the time. Season to taste, stir in the onions and lemon juice, then serve.

MAKES 600 ML / 1 PINT

Cumberland Sauce

A deliciously rich, zesty sauce that is perfect with plain roast
or grilled game

grated rind and juice of 1 orange
grated rind and juice of 1 lemon
75ml/5tbsp water
75ml/5tbsp port
30ml/2tbsp vinegar
100g/4oz redcurrant jelly
1.25ml/¼ tsp prepared English mustard
salt
pinch of cayenne pepper

Put the orange and lemon rind into a small saucepan with the water and heat to simmering point. Simmer gently for 10 minutes. Add the port, vinegar, redcurrant jelly and mustard, then heat gently until the jelly melts. Add the orange and lemon juice to the pan with the seasoning. Simmer for 3–4 minutes.

Serve hot or cold with roast game.

MAKES ABOUT 250 ML / 8 FL OZ

Piquant Sauce

1 small onion or 2 shallots, finely chopped
1 bay leaf
1 blade of mace
30ml/2tbsp vinegar
300ml/½ pint Foundation Brown Sauce
25g/1oz mushrooms, coarsely chopped
15ml/1tbsp capers
15ml/1tbsp gherkins
10ml/2tsp mushroom ketchup
2.5ml/½ tsp sugar (optional)

Put the onion or shallots, bay leaf, mace and vinegar in a saucepan. Heat to boiling point, reduce the heat and simmer for 10 minutes. Heat the sauce, if necessary. Add the onion mixture and the mushrooms to the brown sauce, then simmer for about 15 minutes, until the mushrooms are softened.

Meanwhile, halve the capers and chop the gherkins. Remove the bay leaf and mace from the sauce and add the capers, gherkins, mushroom ketchup and sugar, if used. Reheat if required.

MAKES ABOUT 300 ML / ½ PINT

Mushroom Sauce

15–25g/½–1oz butter
50–100g/2–4oz button mushrooms, thinly slices
White sauce made with 15g/½oz butter, 15g/½oz flour and 250ml/8floz milk

Melt the butter in a pan, add the mushrooms and cook gently for 15 – 20 minutes. Heat the sauce; stir in the mushrooms and their juices.

MAKES ABOUT 250 ML / 8 FL OZ

Top: Jellied Game Salad (page 152); Below: Terrine of Duck (page 149)

Oyster Sauce

8–10 large fresh oysters or 1 (225g/8oz) can oysters (not smoked oysters)
275ml/9fl oz fish stock
salt and pepper • lemon juice

Open the fresh oysters, if used. Strain the liquor from the shells and add it to the fish stock. Reserve 6 oysters. Heat the stock gently to simmering point, add all except the reserved oysters and simmer for 10 minutes. Strain the stock and use to make a white sauce (see Mushroom sauce, page 166). Cut the reserved oysters into 3–4 pieces. Add to the hot sauce and simmer for 3–4 minutes. Season and add lemon juice to taste.

If using canned oysters, drain the liquid from the can and add it to the fish stock. Simmer the stock until reduced to 250ml/8fl oz. Strain, and use to make the white sauce. Cut 6–8 oysters into 3–4 pieces. Add them to the hot sauce and simmer for 2–3 minutes. Season and add lemon juice.

MAKES ABOUT 600 ML / 1 PINT

Fresh Tomato Sauce

1 onion, finely chopped
1 garlic clove, crushed (optional)
1 rasher rindless streaky bacon, chopped
30ml/2 tbsp olive oil
800g/1¾ lb tomatoes, peeled and chopped
salt and pepper • pinch of sugar
5ml/1 tsp chopped fresh basil (optional)

Fry the onion, garlic and bacon in the oil for 5 minutes. Add the rest of the ingredients, cover and simmer gently for 30 minutes. Rub through a sieve or process in an electric blender until smooth.

MAKES ABOUT 600 ML / 1 PINT

Prune Sauce

225g/8oz prunes
300ml/½pint water
strip of lemon rind • 25g/1oz sugar
pinch of ground cinnamon
15ml/1tbsp rum or brandy (optional)
lemon juice

Soak the prunes in the water overnight. Put them into a saucepan with the lemon rind and stew until tender. Remove the stones and lemon rind, then rub the prunes and liquid through a sieve, or process in an electric blender until smooth. Reheat and add the sugar, cinnamon, rum or brandy, if used, and lemon juice to taste.

M A K E S A B O U T 3 5 0 M L / 1 2 F L O Z

Bigarade Sauce

½ Seville orange
juice of ½ lemon
250ml/8fl oz Espagnole Sauce (page 162)
60ml/4tbsp red wine (optional)
5ml/1tsp redcurrant jelly
salt • cayenne pepper
sugar

Pare the orange rind and cut into neat, thin strips. Put them in a saucepan and cover with a little cold water. Heat to simmering point and cook until just tender. Drain. Squeeze the juice from the orange. Add to the Espagnole Sauce with the orange rind and lemon juice. Reheat the sauce. Stir in the wine, if used, and the redcurrant jelly. Add salt, cayenne and sugar to taste.

M A K E S A B O U T 3 0 0 M L / ½ P I N T

Cooked Red Wine Marinade

1 carrot, thinly sliced
1 onion, thinly sliced
1.1litres/2pints water
3 bay leaves
12 black peppercorns
15ml/1tbsp salt
250ml/8fl oz red wine
juice of 1 lemon
5ml/1tsp granulated sugar
6 juniper berries

Put the carrot and onion in a saucepan with the water, bay leaves, peppercorns and salt, then cook until the vegetables are tender.

When cooked, add the rest of the ingredients. Put the meat or game in a basin and pour the hot marinade over it. Marinate for as long as required, turning over the meat frequently. For a large piece of meat left to soak for 36 hours or longer, strain off the marinade on the second day. Reboil it and leave to cool completely, then pour it back over the meat. This can be done a second time over a 4–5 day period, if required. The marinade should not be reboiled more than twice.

MAKES ABOUT 1.25 LITRES / 2¼ PINTS

Duchesse Potatoes

450g/1lb old potatoes
25g/1oz butter or margarine
1 egg or 2 egg yolks
salt and pepper
a little freshly grated nutmeg (optional)
butter or margarine for greasing
a little beaten egg for brushing

Set the oven at 400°F/200°C/gas 6. Boil or steam the potatoes for about 20 minutes, or until tender. Drain thoroughly and sieve. Beat in the fat and egg or egg yolks. Season to taste with salt and pepper and add the nutmeg, if used. Allow the potatoes to cool slightly.

Spoon the mixture into a piping bag fitted with a large nozzle and pipe rounds of potato on to a greased baking tray. Gently brush the piped potato with a little beaten egg. Bake for about 15 minutes, or until the potatoes are a good golden-brown, then serve at once.

MAKES ABOUT 450G/1LB

Red Wine Marinade

1 onion, chopped
1 carrot, chopped
1 celery stick, chopped
6–10 parsley sprigs, chopped
1 garlic clove, crushed
5ml/1tsp dried thyme
1 bay leaf
6–8 peppercorns
1–2 cloves
2.5ml/1/2 tsp ground coriander
2.5ml/1/2 tsp juniper berries
salt and pepper
250ml/8fl oz All-purpose Stock (page 40)
150ml/1/4 pint red wine
150ml/1/4 pint water
150ml/1/4 pint sunflower oil

Mix all the ingredients in a large bowl, then use as required.

MAKES ABOUT 600ML/1PINT

Macédoine of Vegetables

1 turnip
100g/4oz carrot • 225g/8oz potatoes
750ml/1¼ pints water • 5ml/1 tsp salt
a few runner beans
a few cauliflower florets
225g/8oz fresh peas
25–50g/1–2oz butter • pepper

Cut the turnip, carrots and poatoes into 1 cm/½ inch dice. Cut the beans into 1 cm/½ inch diamond shapes. Bring the water to the boil and add the salt. Put in the turnip and carrots, then boil for 3 minutes. Add the beans and boil for another 3 minutes, then add the remaining vegetables. Boil for 5–10 minutes, until tender. Drain and toss in the butter and pepper.

MAKES ABOUT 700G / 1 ½ LB

Basic Forcemeat and Forcemeat Balls

50g/2oz margarine or shredded suet
100g/4oz fresh breadcrumbs
pinch of freshly grated nutmeg
15ml/1tbsp chopped parsley
5ml/1tsp chopped fresh mixed herbs
grated rind of ½ lemon
salt and pepper • 1 egg

Set the oven at 350°F/180°C/gas 4, if baking. Melt the margarine, if using. Mix all the ingredients thoroughly.

To make Forcemeat Balls, form the mixture into 12 or 16 balls and bake for 15–20 minutes, or fry in deep or shallow fat until golden.

MAKES 12 TO 16 BALLS

Glossary

Aspic Savoury jelly made from meat, fish or poultry stock and gelatine.

Bacon rolls Rindless bacon rashers, rolled and skewered, then baked or grilled until brown.

Bain-marie Large, container filled with hot water into which a smaller container can be placed during cooking.

Bard To cover delicate or dry meat, poultry or game with thin slices of pork fat or fat bacon during cooking.

Baron Baron of hare is the body section without the head, neck or limbs.

Bat To beat out a thin slice of meat into a larger, thinner slice, also tenderising it.

Beurre manié Equal quantities of butter and flour kneaded into a paste. Used for thickening soups, sauces and stews.

Bouquet garni Small bunch of herbs, including parsley sprigs, thyme and bay.

Braise A gentle, moist cooking method, using a little liquid in a covered pot.

Clarify To remove the impurities from fat by heating then straining through muslin.

Civet Game casserole using a marinade and often the blood of the animal.

Croûte Round, rectangular or triangular piece of toasted or fried bread.

Croûtons Small dice of fried or toasted bread used as a garnish.

Deglaze Also known by the French term, *déglacer*. To boil liquid with pan juices after cooking.

Demi-glace Well-reduced Espagnole Sauce with the juices from roasted meat added.

Draw To remove the head, neck, feet and viscera from poultry and game.

Dress To pluck, draw and truss game.

Flame To ignite alcohol poured over food during or after cooking.

Fleurons Small, half-moon shapes of puff pastry used as a garnish.

Forcemeat Stuffing.

French dressing Dressing of half or two-thirds oil to vinegar. Season with salt, pepper, mustard and sugar.

Fricassée Velouté or white stew, usually of chicken, rabbit, lamb or veal.

Fried breadcrumbs Fresh breadcrumbs fried or baked in butter until golden. Seasoned and well drained.

Game chips Very thin slices of potato, washed dried and deep fried until crisp and golden.

Gelatine Setting agent made from animal bones, skin and tissues.

Giblets Neck, gizzard, liver and heart of poultry or game. Can also include head, pinions, feet and kidney.

Giblets gravy Simmer giblets with onion in water for 1½ hours. Strain and boil stock with meat cooking juices. Season and strain.

Glaze To coat food with beaten egg, milk, aspic or meat glaze.

Hang To suspend game in a cool, airy place in order to tenderise the meat and give it the characteristic gamey flavour.

Joint To divide game into serving pieces by severing the joints.

Jugged dishes Game in sauce thickened with the blood of the animal.

Lard To thread strips of fat bacon or pork fat through lean meat, poultry and game.

Leveret A hare up to one year old.

Marinate To steep food in a mixture of oil or lemon juice, vinegar or wine and herbs or spices before cooking.

Panada Thick mixture made of flour, butter, seasonings and milk, stock or water.

Paunch To remove the stomach and intestines of a rabbit or hare.

Pluck To remove the feathers from a bird.

Potato straws Cut potatoes into matchstick pieces, wash, dry and deep fry until crisp and golden. Drain well.

Quenelles Smooth, light, oval-shaped dumplings of fish, poultry, game or meat.

Ragoût Well-seasoned, slowly cooked stew

Reduce To evaporate surplus liquid by fast boiling in an uncovered pan.

Roast To cook by dry heat in an oven.

Roux Equal quantities of fat and flour cooked together, used to thicken sauces.

Salmi Casserole made from game or poultry in which the birds are partially roasted, then cooked in liquid or a sauce.

Sauté To fry food rapidly in shallow fat until brown, turning all the time.

Seal or sear To brown the surface of food in hot fat or in a hot oven to seal it and retain all the juices.

Simmer To heat liquid until boiling point, then reduce the heat to keep the liquid just below boiling point, over a gentle heat.

Sippets Pieces of toast cut into fingers, triangles and other shapes.

Skewer To pass a metal spike through meat or to thread food onto it.

Skim To remove surface fat, scum or cream from a liquid.

Stew To cook in plenty of liquid in a covered pan.

Sweat To gently cook vegetables in a little fat in a covered pan.

Terrine Earthenware dish in which pâtés are cooked. Also the food cooked in it.

Thin gravy Roasting pan juices boiled with stock and strained.

Tomatoes, to peel Cover the tomatoes with freshly boiling water and leave to stand for 30 – 60 seconds. Drain and peel.

Trail Intestines of small game birds.

Truss To tie poultry, meat or game into a neat shape before cooking.

Weight or press To place a weight over a food such as pâté to expel excess moisture and condense the texture of the food.

Index